D0983914

Joseph Conrad:

Language and
Fictional Self-Consciousness

For Dee

Talking to no one is strange;
Talking to someone is stranger,
You might be in danger
If you say too much in this world.

Kevin Coyne

Joseph Conrad:

Language and Fictional Self-Consciousness

Jeremy Hawthorn

The University of Nebraska Press

© Jeremy Hawthorn 1979

First published in the U.S.A. 1979 by
The University of Nebraska Press,
901 North 17th Street, Lincoln, Nebraska 68588

Library of Congress Cataloging in Publication Data

Hawthorn, Jeremy.
    Joseph Conrad: language and fictional self-consciousness.

    Bibliography: p.
    Includes index.
    1. Conrad, Joseph, 1857–1924—Criticism and interpretation.
PR6005.04Z7425   823'.9'12   78–20690

ISBN 0–8032–2305–6

Printed in Great Britain

Contents

Acknowledgements

A number of friends and colleagues read and commented on earlier versions of this book, and I am extremely grateful to all of them for their helpful comments and criticism. I owe a particular debt to Terry Eagleton and Arnold Kettle, who both made extremely useful criticisms of the work, and from whose conversation and writings I have learned much. My debt to Arnold Kettle reaches back to my time as an undergraduate when he was my tutor, through my association with the Open University as a course tutor, and would be hard to exaggerate. All errors and inadequacies in the book are, of course, mine alone.

I must also express my thanks to the following for kind permission to reproduce copyright material:

To Yale University Library, for permission to reproduce excerpts from the manuscripts of Joseph Conrad's *Heart of Darkness* and *Under Western Eyes* in the Beinecke Rare Book and Manuscript Library; to Kevin Coyne and Biscuit Music Ltd for permission to reproduce four lines from 'Talking to No One' by Kevin Coyne; to Faber and Faber Ltd and Harcourt Brace Jovanovich Inc. for permission to reproduce a short extract from 'Gerontion' by T. S. Eliot, published in *Collected Poems 1909–1962*; to Geoffrey Hill, André Deutsch Ltd and Dufour Editions Inc. for permission to reproduce the first fourteen lines of 'September Song' by Geoffrey Hill, published in *King Log*, 1968. I must also thank the Brotherton Library, University of Leeds, for permission to reproduce excerpts from *French Linguistic and Literary Influences on Joseph Conrad* by Yves Hervouet, PhD Thesis, University of Leeds, 1971. I regret that I have not been able to contact Dr Hervouet personally.

Abbreviations

Quotations from Conrad's novels are taken from the Dent Collected Edition, except in the case of *The Shadow-Line* and *Within the Tides*. The volume of the Collected Edition in which these two texts appear is now out of print and unlikely to be reprinted; however, as the Everyman's Library edition of these two texts is still available, and is identical to the Collected Edition text, I have made reference to this below. As some of the volumes in the Collected Edition have been reissued with different pagination the date of each volume referred to should be noted if quotations are to be looked up.

AF   Joseph Conrad, *Almayer's Folly*. Dent Collected Edition, 1947.

APR   Joseph Conrad, *A Personal Record*. Dent Collected Edition, reprinted 1975.

CPB   Zdzistaw Najder (ed.), *Conrad's Polish Background: Letters to and From Polish Friends*. Translated by Halina Carroll, Oxford University Press, London, 1964.

CTAF   Richard Curle (ed.), *Conrad to a Friend: 150 Selected Letters from Joseph Conrad to Richard Curle*. Sampson Low, Marston, London, 1928.

HOD   Joseph Conrad, *Heart of Darkness*. Dent Collected Edition, reprinted 1967.

HODM   Joseph Conrad, holograph of *Heart of Darkness*. Yale University Library.

JCLL I & II   G. Jean-Aubry, *Joseph Conrad: Life and Letters* I and II. Doubleday Page, New York, 1927.

LBM   William Blackburn (ed.), *Joseph Conrad: Letters to William Blackwood and David S. Meldrum*. Duke University Press, Durham, North Carolina, 1958.

LCG   C. T. Watts (ed.), *Joseph Conrad's Letters to R. B. Cunninghame Graham*. Cambridge University Press, London, 1969.

LE   Joseph Conrad, *Last Essays*. Dent Collected Edition,

	reprinted 1972.
LFC	Edward Garnett (ed.), *Letters from Conrad 1895–1924*. Nonesuch Press, London n.d. (1928?).
LJ	Joseph Conrad, *Lord Jim*. Dent Collected Edition, reprinted 1974 (*note*: the initial quotation from Novalis has been omitted from this reprinting).
LJCMP	John A. Gee and Paul J. Sturm (edited and translated by), *Letters of Joseph Conrad to Marguerite Poradowska 1890–1920*. Reprinted by Kennikat Press, Port Washington, New York and London, 1973.
MOS	Joseph Conrad, *The Mirror of the Sea*. Dent Collected Edition, reprinted 1975.
N	Joseph Conrad, *Nostromo*. Dent Collected Edition, reprinted 1975.
NLL	Joseph Conrad, *Notes on Life and Letters*. Dent Collected Edition, reprinted 1970.
NON	Joseph Conrad, *The Nigger of the 'Narcissus'*. Dent Collected Edition, reprinted 1974.
SA	Joseph Conrad, *The Secret Agent*. Dent Collected Edition, reprinted 1974.
SDMPC	A. R. Luria and F. La Yudovitch, *Speech and the Development of Mental Processes in the Child*. Edited by Joan Simon and with a new introduction by James Britton, Penguin, Harmondsworth, reprinted 1975.
SOS	Joseph Conrad, *A Set of Six*. Dent Collected Edition, reprinted 1974.
T	Joseph Conrad, *Typhoon*. Dent Collected Edition, reprinted 1974.
TEOTT	Joseph Conrad, *The End of the Tether*. Dent Collected Edition, reprinted 1967.
TL	L.S. Vygotsky, *Thought and Language*. Translated by Eugenia Hanfmann and Gertrude Vakar, MIT Press, Cambridge Massachusetts, and London, reprinted 1971.
TOU	Joseph Conrad, *Tales of Unrest*. Dent Collected Edition, 1947.
TSL	Joseph Conrad, *The Shadow-Line*. Everyman's Library, London, 1972.
UWE	Joseph Conrad, *Under Western Eyes*. Dent Collected Edition, reprinted 1971.
UWEM	Joseph Conrad, holograph of *Under Western Eyes*, entitled *Razumov* but with *Under Western Eyes* written on the last page. Yale University Library.
WTT	Joseph Conrad, *Within the Tides*. Everyman's Library, London, 1972.

Preface

> Both at sea and on land my point of view is English, from which the
> conclusion should not be drawn that I have become an Englishman.
> That is not the case. Homo duplex has in my case more than one
> meaning. [CPB, 240]

Writing to a Pole and talking about his English point of view,
Conrad doubtless feels particularly strongly that the term 'homo
duplex' is appropriate to describe his situation. But he points
out that the phrase has more than one meaning, and although the
question of nationality is certainly highlighted in the above
quotation, the implication is that there are other ways in which
Conrad feels himself to be a divided man. In the letter from
which this quotation is taken Conrad tells his correspondent that
he has just had to remove the 567th page of the novel on which
he is working in order to "address myself to you". This transition
from novelist to letter writer, from a man addressing many
unknown readers indirectly to a man addressing one particular
person directly, suggests a way in which Conrad might have felt
himself divided which had nothing to do with nationality. The
novelist is, necessarily, a divided person. He or she is known to
his or her acquaintances as a living individual, and to his or her
readers as a more shadowy and indeterminate presence, lurking
in and behind the fictional characters and actions for which he
or she is responsible.

Conrad's major works give evidence not just of the divisions
in Conrad the man, but also of the 'duplicity' of the writer.
They concern themselves with, among other things, the way in
which language in general, and writing in particular, are intimately related to the human ability to be 'duplex', an ability
which allows us to objectify and critically to consider ourselves
and our actions. In *A Personal Record* Conrad testifies to the
writer's inward certitude that literary criticism will never die,
'for man (so variously defined) is, before everything else, a
critical animal' [APR, 96]. To be self-critical we must be able to
objectify part of ourselves: we must, in brief, be 'duplex'.

Literary criticism is thus given a high status by Conrad; it is associated with the critical faculty which sets us apart from animals, the faculty of self-scrutiny.

This faculty, I argue in my introduction, is dependent on, and constituted by, language. Conrad's concern with language is related to many other central concerns in his work, and I hope to be able to demonstrate this through particular analyses of his major works. My view of Conrad's achievement is suggested by the works I have chosen to concentrate upon – *Heart of Darkness*, *Typhoon*, *The Nigger of the 'Narcissus'*, *The Shadow-Line*, *Lord Jim*, *Nostromo*, *The Secret Agent* and *Under Western Eyes*: these, for me, represent the central achievement of Conrad the novelist. I do not find *Victory* a successful work, and I think that *Chance*, although astonishingly worked in its opening hundred or so pages, is a novel vitiated by later failures. Although I have devoted less attention to *Typhoon*, *The Nigger of the 'Narcissus'* and *The Shadow-Line* than to the other works I mention, this should not be taken to suggest that I accord them a lower valuation.

In all of these works Conrad's concern with language is itself duplex. Not only does he see a linguistic element in many of the questions of human identity and behaviour raised by the novels, but these in their turn throw up other questions relating to the novels' own moral justification. As a critical animal himself Conrad not only surveys humanity critically within his novels; he also concerns himself with the status and efficacy of novels and novel writing. Sometimes this is done relatively directly; sometimes it emerges as an indirect concern arising out of a more direct interest in speech or writing.

Critical treatment of Conrad's interest in language has often involved argument about the extent to which he 'chose' to write in English, and the extent to which his other languages influenced his English. Dr Leavis argues that, for all the unidiomatic touches and the suggestions of French yielded by every page of his,

> Conrad's English, as we read his supreme things, compels us to recognize it as that of a highly individual master, who has done his creative thinking and feeling – explored most inwardly the experience leading him to creation – in that language.[1]

I would not wish to offer any substantial disagreement here, although I do feel that close investigation of Conrad's precise debt to Polish and French yields interesting results. So far as French is concerned, Yves Hervouet has shown how often

[1] F. R. Leavis, 'The Shadow-Line', in *'Anna Karenina' and other Essays*, Chatto, London, 1967, p. 94.

Conrad appears to have translated a phrase or expression literally from the French, and there does seem to be evidence for Conrad's having been more influenced by this language when dealing with French-speaking characters. There is also evidence that Conrad switched to French in speech when moved or when expressing ideas, and that in periods of illness he spoke in Polish.[2] But these are facts which do not invalidate Dr Leavis's argument. They do, however, provide us with an explanation of a more than commonly developed consciousness of language on Conrad's part. By this I do not mean a concern with accuracy and precision in expression (although Conrad certainly was so concerned), but more an awakened philosophical curiosity about language, more easily developed perhaps when one speaks and thinks in more than one tongue. General questions about the relationship between thought and language, about the difference between writing and speech, about the oddity of language constituting both a means to communication and also the medium of knowledge, these perhaps all occur more readily to the polyglot, and certainly can be found congealed into the substance of Conrad's fiction. They lead on, almost inevitably, to a curiosity about fiction, about – putting it crudely – what novels are and what they do, and how (or whether) their creation is morally justifiable.

Although I try to introduce relevant social and political ideas and evidence I have not made a study of the overt political statements and opinions in Conrad's novels, letters and essays. This is partly because two comprehensive books on Conrad's politics already exist,[3] and partly because there are, I believe, discontinuities between overt political opinions and underlying meanings in the fiction. I attempt to bring this fact out most directly in my chapter on *Nostromo*.

In my introduction I try to investigate some fundamental questions about the nature of language through an inquiry into Conrad's consciousness and treatment of them in his writings. I hope that this part of the book does not seem too abstract or too far removed from critical discussion of particular texts; apart from a later, short chapter on 'Fiction and truth', in which I look briefly at certain issues raised by my subsequent reading of *Under Western Eyes*, it is the only chapter in the book which does not take the form of a critical discussion of a novel of Conrad's. Although I do sometimes seem to start with theoretical

2 Yves Hervouet, *French Linguistic and Literary Influences on Joseph Conrad*. PhD thesis, University of Leeds, 1971, pp. 42–55.
3 Avrom Fleishman, *Conrad's Politics*. John Hopkins, Baltimore, 1967. Eloise Knapp Hay, *The Political Novels of Joseph Conrad*. University of Chicago Press, Chicago and London, reprinted 1972.

discussion, or with abstractions, my main concerns in this book
have been developed from reading Conrad's novels.

Introduction: language and self-consciousness

Introducing the volume of letters from Conrad that he edited, David Garnett remarks that Conrad's Congo experiences were the turning point in his mental life, their effects on him determining his transformation from a sailor to a writer. He continues:

> According to his emphatic declaration to me in his early years at sea he had 'not a thought in his head'. 'I was a perfect animal', he reiterated, meaning, of course, that he had reasoned and reflected hardly at all over all the varieties of life he had encountered. [LFC, xii]

G. Jean-Aubry, in his *Joseph Conrad in the Congo*, repeats this anecdote, with the slight alteration that Conrad is reported to have called himself a simple, rather than a perfect animal. Jean-Aubry glosses the remark in a similar way to Garnett, suggesting that Conrad wished to convey that during the first fifteen years of navigation (prior to his Congo experiences),

> [he] lived almost without noticing it, led away by the fire of his temperament, drawn by an almost unconscious desire for adventure, without ever reflecting on the reasons for his activity or that of anyone else. [1]

Jean-Aubry's gloss, although similar to Garnett's, includes a significant extension: the difference between the pre-Congo Conrad and the post-Congo Conrad is not just that the latter reflected more over the varieties of life he encountered, but that he moved from unconsciousness of himself and his own activity, to an awareness of himself and to a realization that the reasons for his own activity could be scrutinized. As Garnett suggests, this change is intimately involved in Conrad's transformation from sailor to writer.

Conrad himself refers to a comparable dawning of self-consciousness in his author's note to *The Shadow-Line*. The moment of awakening self-consciousness here is located at a different time in Conrad's life, however, in the period of his first command.

1 G. Jean-Aubry, *Joseph Conrad in the Congo*. 'The Bookman's Journal' Office, London, 1926, p. 73.

Primarily the aim of this piece of writing was the presentation of certain facts which certainly were associated with the change from youth, care-free and fervent, to the more self-conscious and more poignant period of maturer life. [TSL, vi]

The fact that Conrad does fix the dawning of his self-consciousness at different times is not just an example of his notorious unreliability in matters concerning his own history. It is also a reminder that self-consciousness is not a single event, but a process which stretches over time, continually developing and consolidating itself. I think, in fact, that there are several stages in Conrad's life – and more particularly, in Conrad's development as a writer – which can be fixed as points where he became conscious of himself and his own activity. As Conrad admits on several occasions, to be a writer of fiction is to engage in a more self-conscious activity than to be a sailor; it is however also true that within Conrad's work we can see the development of an increasingly self-conscious attitude towards his craft itself. More and more Conrad's novels concern themselves with the nature of language, the status of fiction, and at a higher level still, the whole question of self-consciousness, of man's ability to scrutinize himself and his activity.

I want, in the pages that follow, to try to look at what I consider to be Conrad's major works while plotting this developing self-consciousness within them. There is, I hasten to add, no neat or easy progression. In general terms, though, I think that a movement from an early fascination with language, both spoken and written, through to a concern with the relationship between 'mental' and 'real' events, culminating in a concern with fiction and self-consciousness as subjects for enquiry, can be detected in Conrad's writing.

There are two questions raised by the foregoing which at this point demand some preliminary consideration: what are the distinguishing features of self-consciousness, and what are the forces that call it into being? I am not qualified to write as a philosopher on such questions, but I think that it is possible to suggest answers to both of them, answers which are not easily separable. To be perhaps aggressively blunt and unphilosophical, I would suggest that self-consciousness involves separation from something which hitherto was considered to be a part of oneself – an objectification of something previously experienced subjectively – and that self-consciousness occurs precisely when forces compel a person, a group, or an age to engage in such an objectification. We become self-conscious, in a profound as well as a simple way, when we view from outside that which previously we have taken for granted. This can happen to an individual, as it happened to Conrad in the Congo, or it can happen to a whole society at certain points in history. At the start of his essay 'The Unlighted Coast', in which he writes of the experience of landing in an England darkened, literally and metaphorically, by the war, Conrad notes that 'life had never before perhaps in the history of that unlighted island known such an intense consciousness of itself.'

Conrad was not, in Eliot's words, 'assured of certain certainties', and Najder has pointed out how his separation from the unconsidered assumptions of many of his adopted countrymen allowed him to see things to which they were blind:

> He was an isolated man, but this very isolation, making him feel disturbed and insecure, at the same time made it possible for him to see problems which escaped many writers more tightly entangled in the prevailing social conditions. [CPB, 31]

What I want to draw particular attention to is the way in which the uniqueness of human language is involved in a fundamental way in man's ability to separate himself from part of himself, to objectify his own experience. The distinction drawn by Conrad, between himself as 'perfect animal' without a thought in his head and himself as thinking, self-scrutinizing human being, draws attention to language, for a key distinction between animals and human beings is that the former lack language. Engels, in his unfinished work on *The Part Played by Labour in the Transition from Ape to Man*, refers to this specific difference:

> Animals communicate in many ways, but their communication is limited to reactions to the immediate situation – to warnings of danger, sexual invitations, challenges, and the like. Language involves being able to detach the communication from the immediate situation, through assigning to arbitrary clusters of sounds specific meanings to do not only with objects, acts, and feelings, but also with things and events of the past and the future, both possible and impossible.[2]

'Being able to detach the communication from the immediate situation' is analogous to what I inelegantly referred to as separating oneself from part of oneself. Language can scrutinize itself precisely because it has an arbitrary quality; animal 'language', in contrast, is 'non-displaced', it arises out of here-and-now situations of which it forms a part and from which it cannot be separated. Animals cannot communicate about danger or hunger (excepting the special case of play) unless they feel threatened or are hungry; human beings can talk about such topics in isolation

2 F. Engels, 'The Part Played by Labor in the Transition from Ape to Man'. Printed as an appendix in F. Engels, *The Origin of the Family, Private Property and the State*, Lawrence and Wishart, London, 1972, p. 254.

from actual danger or hunger, and can go further to talk of the words which refer to danger or hunger, or can manipulate them so as to produce new meanings – as in 'I feel threatened by love.' The animal *cannot* become self-conscious in the way that a human being can; as Marx expresses it, the animal does not distinguish itself from its life activity, it *is* its life activity.[3] Through language, and the mental operations which it makes possible, human beings can distinguish themselves from their life activity, can reflect on the reasons for their activity or the activity of others.

James Britton, introducing Luria and Yudovich's classic study, *Speech and the Development of Mental Processes in the Child*, shows how language allows human beings to escape from imprisonment in concrete experience. In illustration of this he contrasts the behaviour of two-year-old Alison with that of four-year-old Clare during a period of fifteen minutes. In the course of this time

> Clare, sat on the sofa with coloured pencils and a drawing block and, in spite of interruptions from Alison, the younger child, she completed two pictures; one of a girl riding a pony and one of a girl diving into a pool – both of them references back to things she had seen and done on her summer holiday three months earlier. She talked to herself from time to time about what she was doing. [SDMPC, 11]

Over the same period of time, Britton notes, her younger sister went through a succession of unconnected activities ranging from pretending to be a goat to crawling under the table to claim Britton's pen and taking the lace out of a shoe she sees. Britton concludes:

> It will be clear I think that Alison's behaviour arises almost entirely in response to the various stimuli of the here and now, and is in this respect in direct contrast to Clare's sustained activity. [SDMPC, 12]

Language is thus the means whereby self-consciousness can be obtained, as it enables human beings to progress beyond a purely sensory relationship with the world to a conscious and critically aware one.

Two points need to be added here – firstly, as I have already argued, that the achievement of self-consciousness is not a once-for-all step, but a process which can continue indefinitely, as consciousness displaces itself from itself and examines itself; and secondly that such displacement brings on the one hand freedom from the concrete and greater power over it, but also greater vulnerability to error and deception.

3 Karl Marx, *Economic and Philosophical Manuscripts of 1844*. Lawrence and Wishart, London 1970, p. 113.

Let me take the first of these two points. When Conrad described himself as a 'perfect animal', he was of course speaking metaphorically. He could speak when he went to the Congo, and the gift of speech meant that he already had the ability at one level to escape from concrete experience. But what I would argue is that the jump of self-consciousness engendered by his Congo experiences is *comparable* to the jump from the position of imprisonment in the concrete to a position of a relative independence of immediate concrete experience that the child achieves through the acquisition of speech. Conrad's achievement of self-consciousness subsequent to his Congo experiences is the achievement of self-consciousness at a different level from that achieved by the child Clare. Clare has, through language, managed to move for the first time from immersion in activity to the scrutiny of that same activity. Conrad, after the Congo, manages to objectify certain specifically political or ideological aspects of his previous experiences. First-hand acquaintance with the brutalities of imperialist exploitation forces him to consider assumptions and activities which he had previously *lived* rather than *considered*.

Gregory Bateson, in his essay, 'A Theory of Play and Fantasy', suggests:

> It is evident that a very important stage [in the evolution of communication] occurs when the organism gradually ceases to respond quite 'automatically' to the mood-signs of another and becomes able to recognize the sign as a signal: that is, to recognize that the other individual's and its own signals are only signals, which can be trusted, distrusted, falsified, denied, amplified, corrected and so forth.[4]

Although Bateson is talking about an evolutionary stage in the development of a species, it seems apparent that what he says could apply to different stages of an individual's development too, and that 'recognizing the sign as a sign' can be an important stage in the development of a critical intelligence. Bateson also compares messages to mathematical equations which can always be put in new brackets, or qualifiers which alter the tenor of the message, and he argues that just as a mathematician can go on adding more and more brackets, so too can human beings continue to re-examine aspects of their concrete experience through more and more abstract discussion. I would suggest that few writers are more conscious than Conrad that a word is only a word, and can be trusted, distrusted, falsified, denied, amplified and corrected.

4 Gregory Bateson, 'A Theory of Play and Fantasy'. Reprinted in *Steps to an Ecology of Mind*, Paladin edn, Frogmore, St Albans, 1973, p. 151.

Jerome Bruner, in his very interesting introduction to L.S. Vygotsky's *Thought and Language*, draws attention to Vygotsky's emphasis on 'man's capacity to create higher order structures that, in effect, replace and give new power to the conceptual structures that one climbed over en route to higher order mastery'. As with Bateson's mathematical analogy this formulation posits a hierarchy of more and more 'detached' abstractions which incorporate and subtly modify earlier formulations. Vygotsky himself gives us examples of such hierarchical jumps – when the child, for example, realizes that a word is something separate from what it names, rather than an attribute or a property of what it refers to. A similar jump on a higher level occurs when we move from speech to writing. Vygotsky points out that even the minimal development of writing

> requires a high level of abstraction. It is speech in thought and image only, lacking the musical, expressive, intonational qualities of oral speech. . . . Writing is also speech without an interlocutor, addressed to an absent or an imaginary person or to no one in particular . . . . The motives for writing are more abstract, more intellectualized, further removed from immediate needs. [TL, 98, 99]

The distinction between writing and speech is one of which Conrad is very conscious, and one to which he attaches much significance. In particular, as I will go on to argue in the next chapter, he is aware of the fact that although writing allows human beings to escape from the concrete, this ability can bring with it either more power or more vulnerability to error. Kurtz, we can recall, had 'kicked himself loose of the earth', and as a result undoubtedly gained power over many of his fellow human beings; but he ends up crawling on the ground on all-fours, appalled by what he has seen and done. For Conrad the sign, and in particular the word, is a fascinating and complex thing, and the relationship between sign and referent engages his almost obsessive attention. At one time the sign seems divorced from reality, telling lies; at another it appears more mighty than the sword, precipitating events which are tragically concrete and have, to use a phrase of his own, 'no sham meaning' [SOS, 78]. In the course of his investigation into the nature of the sign Conrad asks questions not just about language, but about that professional usage of language which constitutes fiction. What his finest novels present us with is more than an investigation into the nature of human beings and of their language: it is a consideration of the novels' own ontology – a probing enquiry into the sort of truth which can be found 'at the heart of fiction' [NLL, 6].

1

Heart of Darkness:
language and truth

> The word within a word, unable to speak a word,
> Swaddled with darkness. [T. S. Eliot, 'Gerontion']

There are two pieces of writing to which the attention of the
reader of *Heart of Darkness* is drawn, and the differences between
the two can stand as evidence of Conrad's perception of the
power of language in general, and writing in particular, to build
or to betray. About half way through the novel Marlow notes
almost as an aside that the International Society for the Sup-
pression of Savage Customs had entrusted Kurtz with the
making of a report for its future guidance.

> And he had written it, too. I've seen it. I've read it. It was eloquent,
> vibrating with eloquence, but too high-strung, I think. Seventeen
> pages of close writing he had found time for! But this must have been
> before his – let us say – nerves, went wrong, and caused him to preside
> at certain midnight dances ending with unspeakable rites, which – as
> far as I reluctantly gathered from what I heard at various times – were
> offered up to him – do you understand? – to Mr Kurtz himself. But it
> was a beautiful piece of writing. [HOD, 117]

The irony of the passage is bitter and fundamental, involving
not only Kurtz, but Marlow and, we may perhaps feel, Conrad
himself. The gap between the 'eloquent' report and the 'unspeakable' rites is crucial to this irony, and helps us to an initial
understanding of Conrad's suspicion of language in general and
'beautiful writing' in particular. 'Eloquent' is a word he hardly
ever uses innocently: by it he nearly always implies a morally
suspect facility with words, an ability to build beautiful verbal
structures which are at variance with what is really the case. The
passage above encapsulates a sick fear to be found at the heart of
much of Conrad's own writing – a fear of the lure and charm of
beautiful writing which, like Dorian Gray's portrait, is beautiful
to the extent that it is untrue.

Indeed, 'eloquent', for Conrad, is almost an interchangable
term for 'skilful lying'. In his first published novel, *Almayer's*

Folly, we are given an account of a long piece of such skilful lying by the character Babalatchi, whose name is perhaps intended to suggest the curse of Babel. Babalatchi, we are told, 'was eloquent and persuasive, calling heaven and earth to witness the truth of his statements'. Unfortunately, as Marlow reminds us at the end of *Heart of Darkness*, heaven does not manifest its recognition of such falsehoods.

The need to distinguish between writing fiction and telling lies seems to have been a recurrent problem for Conrad. He often refers to the writing of fiction in terms of purveying untruths, and it is not always easy to assess the extent to which such statements involve self-mockery. Writing to R. B. Cunninghame Graham on 1 May 1898 – the year *Heart of Darkness* was published – Conrad noted sarcastically:

> My own life is difficult enough. It arises from the fact that there is nothing handy to steal and I never could invent an effective lie – a lie that would sell, and last, and be admirable. [LCG, 85]

Kurtz's report does not exactly sell, but in as much as it is vibrating with eloquence it is admirable, and Marlow tells Kurtz's Intended that Kurtz's words will last. I don't think that it is too far-fetched, therefore, to see in Conrad's treatment of the report a vein of questioning which relates to *Heart of Darkness* itself and to the writing of fiction in general. Conrad was fond of playing on the two meanings of the word 'fiction' and at times it seems as if he feared that the two meanings were but one.

> The best of them [the Roman invaders of Britain] is they didn't get up pretty fictions about it. Was there, I wonder, an association on a philanthropic basis to develop Britain, with some third rate thing for a president? [HODM, 15]

The quotation is from Conrad's manuscript of *Heart of Darkness* and does not appear in the published version. The ambiguity of 'getting up pretty fictions' is instructive. It can mean the creation of 'effective lies', or fictional accounts in the form of novels based on imperialist experiences. Conrad himself has 'got up a fiction' about his experiences in Africa: what perhaps exercises him here is whether his fiction is any truer than is Kurtz's piece of beautiful writing. Telling lies and writing novels are activities related by their mutual reliance upon the arbitrary nature of the sign – the 'portability' of the word.

I mentioned two pieces of writing in *Heart of Darkness* however, and if Kurtz's report is exemplary of Conrad's awareness of the way written words can lie and mislead, *An Inquiry into Some Points of Seamanship* – the book Marlow finds and returns to the young Russian – is in contrast testimony to

Conrad's recognition that written words are also possessed of a potentiality for honest reportage. Referring to this book Marlow notes that it was not

> a very enthralling book; but at the first glance you could see there a singleness of intention, an honest concern for the right way of going to work, which made these humble pages, thought out so many years ago, luminous with another than a professional light. The simple old sailor, with his talk of chains and purchases, made me forget the jungle and the pilgrims in a delicious sensation of having come upon something unmistakably real. [HOD, 99]

If the word 'eloquence' is a mark of the dishonesty of Kurtz's report, 'work', and perhaps 'simple' have the opposite effect here. Work for Conrad is at the centre of moral reliability: through work human beings (or men, as Conrad usually expresses the matter) find out the truth. It is work which acts as the reliable mediator between what people think and what is actually the case; as I shall argue later Conrad usually means by this, however, physical work of the sort a sailor engages in – a writer's work may be equally demanding in different ways but its rewards in terms of achieved truth are less guaranteed. In his 'Memorandum On the Scheme for Fitting Out a Sailing Ship for the Purpose of Perfecting the Training of Merchant Service Officers Belonging to the Port of Liverpool', Conrad spends a full page and a half in arguing that the proposed ship should carry no labour-saving appliances. His points in favour of his position on this matter are interesting – that the boys will be up to the work, that such work should not be seen as beneath the dignity of aspiring officers, that there is something elevating in physical work 'into which one puts all one's heart in association with others and for a clearly understood purpose', and finally that 'any physical work intelligently done develops a special mentality; in this case it would be the sailor mentality' |LE, 70|.

What Conrad calls the sailor mentality is strongly apparent in the description of *An Inquiry into Some Points of Seamanship*. The 'singleness of intention' to be found in the book (reminiscent perhaps of the qualities of Singleton in *The Nigger of the 'Narcissus'*) can be compared with the 'clearly understood purpose' which, in his 'Memorandum', Conrad argues should lie behind collective physical endeavour. Through Marlow's relief at discovering the *Inquiry* we sense Conrad's respect for written language (although it is interesting that the above passage refers to 'talk') which is used as a precise tool, language which has been forged through direct contact with physical reality in the work process and which has as a result the same unproblematic relationship with reality that the tool has with the material for which it is designed and the characteristics of which its design reflects.

Conrad hated journalism, and it seems likely that this was because 'journalese' was the absolute antithesis of precise technical language. In *The Mirror of the Sea* Conrad contrasts these two varieties of language, and his argument has I think a direct relevance to the implied distinction he makes between the two pieces of writing in *Heart of Darkness*:

> Your journalist, whether he takes charge of a ship or a fleet, almost invariably 'casts' his anchor. Now, an anchor is never cast, and to take a liberty with technical language is a crime against the clearness, precision, and beauty of perfected speech.
>
> An anchor is a forged piece of iron, admirably adapted to its end, and technical language is an instrument wrought into perfection by ages of experience, a flawless thing for its purpose. [MOS, 13]

'Experience' here performs a similar task to that performed by 'work' in the description of the *Inquiry*; it guarantees that the language will bring to the reader's mind something 'unmistakably real', something true. The thing about technical language is that it has what one can call a reciprocal relationship with reality: a particular need creates the term, and the term is then used whenever that need recurs. Journalism, as Conrad pointed out on several occasions, involved the use of words and phrases which could be used for almost any occasion, and for the journalist it was thus a recommendation that a term did *not* call to mind a particular reality.

Words, then, need not be constitutive of merely 'pretty fictions', they can call to mind 'something unmistakably real'. In many ways it seems true to say that much of Conrad's fiction and non-fiction is devoted to an exploration of this janus-faced character of words. Conrad consistently associates the language of sailors with a direct and non-problematic relationship with reality: 'there is no mystification in the language of truth contained in the Notices to Mariners' [LE, 40]. In his essay 'The Unlighted Coast', he contrasts the 'war talk' of 'men (and even great men)', who we presume are not engaged in actually fighting, with the 'war talk' of sailors on active service, which is

> full of sense, of meaning, and single-minded purpose; inquiries, information, orders, reports. Words, too. But words in direct relation to things and facts, with the feeling at the back of it all of the correct foresight that planned and of the determination which carries on the protective work. [LE, 50]

'Work', again – and also 'single-minded purpose', in direct line of descent, surely, from the 'singleness of purpose' of the *Enquiry*.[1]

At the heart of Conrad's distinction between the reliability of 'words in direct relation to things and facts' and the unreliability of 'eloquence', simple though it may seem, lies a profound perception. Words, unlike the call-signs of animals, do not always have a direct relation to things and facts. Naming is only one aspect of language, and indeed, were it not then language would not be the flexible tool it is, would not give human beings the control over themselves and their world that they alone have. Claire and W. M. S. Russell, in their article 'Language and Animal Signs', point out how perfectly adapted to particular tasks the communication systems of creatures such as bees are. But this precision is also an inflexibility: a bee can return to the hive and signal the presence of pollen to the hive's inhabitants with astonishing accuracy; but when bees are given food at the top of a radio mast they are incapable of communicating this unusual location of food to their fellows. The Russells make similar points about the communication systems of dolphins and chimpanzees. Man, in contrast, has a communication system – word language – that is not only capable of precise adaptation to particular tasks, but is also flexible enough to adapt to new and hitherto unexperienced situations, or even to consider such situations before they occur. In addition, they argue, true language

> involves the free combination of symbols limited only by logical rules of grammar and syntax, which themselves express *relations between* symbols and hence symbolize *relations between* things and individuals and events.[2]

As Conrad is clearly aware, language can be used – is often used – in such a way that *words are in direct relation to things and facts*. But language also has much higher-level capacities, where the semiotic relationship is not between a word and a fact, but between *relations between words*, and *relations between things, individuals, and events*. This higher-level capacity undoubtedly, as the Russells state, brings with it a revolutionizing accession of power over nature and over themselves to human beings; but as Conrad points out, it also brings with it vulnerabilities and dangers.

Before returning to *Heart of Darkness* I would like to make

1 Quoting from *The Secret Sharer*, Dr Leavis comments that '"singleness" turns out to be peculiarly a telling word'; the quotation refers to the 'untempted life' of the sea and 'the singleness of its purpose', [Leavis, *op. cit.*, p. 113].

2 Noel Minnis (ed.), *Linguistics at Large*. Paladin edn, Frogmore, St Albans, 1973, p. 167.

brief reference to Conrad's discussion of language in a nautical context in both *The Nigger of the 'Narcissus' and Typhoon.* Singleton, in *The Nigger of the 'Narcissus'*, is referred to as 'a child', like the other sailors. We are told that although he reads the 'polished and so curiously insincere sentences' of Bulwer Lytton,

> The thoughts of all his lifetime could have been expressed in six words, but the stir of those things that were as much part of his existence as his beating heart called up a gleam of alert understanding upon the sternness of his aged face. [NON, 26]

We can recall Conrad's statement, reported by Garnett, that as a sailor he himself had had 'not a thought in his head' in his early years at sea. Singleton is described by Conrad as having only such thoughts as could have been expressed in six words (which, we need to remember, could be a comment on his thoughts, or on words, or on both). I think that it is instructive to compare the statement that 'the stir of those things . . . were as much part of his existence as his beating heart' with Marx's comment on the distinction between human beings and animals, to which I have already referred. For Marx,

> The animal is immediately one with its life activity. It does not distinguish itself from it. It is *its life activity*. Man makes his life activity itself the object of his will and of his consciousness.[3]

Man, in other words, is self-conscious in a way that the animal or the child is not – and it is Singleton's lack of self-consciousness that merits his being referred to as a child by Conrad. It is fitting that when on shore, separate from part of his existence – his life activity – Singleton is normally paralytically drunk and incapable of distinguishing daylight. Small wonder that Conrad treated with scorn the suggestion that an 'educated Singleton' was other than a contradiction in terms: a self-conscious Singleton would not be Singleton. Singleton is more a part of the world than in a particular relationship with it, as in order to have a relationship with the world he would have to, in some way, distinguish himself from it. That he does not so distinguish himself is closely related to the unverbalized nature of his experience and activity.

In *Typhoon*, a book of seamanship performs a comparable function to that which it is given in *Heart of Darkness*. Reading the book on storms the dogged MacWhirr is at first lost 'amongst advancing semi-circles, left- and right-hand quadrants, the curves of the tracks, the probable bearing of the centre, the shifts

3 See page 4, note 3.

of wind and the readings of the barometer'. MacWhirr has already been introduced to readers as a man who, if not a part of his life-activity, is certainly firmly anchored in the actual:

> The past being to his mind done with, and the future not there yet, the more general actualities of the day required no comment – because facts can speak for themselves with overwhelming precision. [T, 9]

A book which deals with the possible rather than the actual, and which deals with it in terms of abstractions such as 'advancing semi-circles', not surprisingly causes him difficulties, especially when he tries as it were to 'concretize' the abstractions he finds:

> He tried to bring all these things into a definite relation to himself, and ended by becoming contemptuously angry with such a lot of words and with so much advice, all headwork and supposition, without a glimmer of certitude. [T, 33]

But of course, abstractions do not have a definite relation to particular individuals, nor do they provide certitude in particular cases. MacWhirr's attitude to words is to a degree comparable to Singleton's, but not wholly, as we shall see. His letters home are exclusively factual, he is – we are to presume – impervious to his father's 'sly chaffing', and he cannot understand Jukes's objections to the flag they are flying. Jukes, of course, objects to it because it is not a British flag; MacWhirr interprets his objection in a completely different way:

> 'There's nothing amiss with that flag.'
> 'Isn't there?' mumbled Jukes, falling on his knees before a deck-locker and jerking therefrom viciously a spare lead-line.
> 'No. I looked up the book. Length twice the breadth and the elephant exactly in the middle. I thought the people ashore would know how to make the local flag. Stands to reason. You were wrong, Jukes....' [T, 10]

Apart from providing us with charming evidence that Conrad had a developed sense of humour and could write delicately amusing passages as well as he could more sombre pieces, the scene warns us that although MacWhirr's imagination is limited, it is not so limited as Singleton's. He can make use of a book – and his narrow imagination turns out to be of more use in the typhoon than Jukes's more metaphysical speculations about national identity. (His apparently carping objections to the bad lock at the start of the story are similarly seen to be well founded by the end.) MacWhirr, we are told, treats words in his letters to his wife as if they were 'worn-out things, and of a faded meaning', but on the other hand the 'eloquent facts' of the China Seas, which 'speak to a seaman in clear and definite language', 'appealed to Captain MacWhirr's sense of realities so forcibly that he had given up his state-room below and practically lived all his days on the bridge of the ship'. Like the Assistant Commissioner in *The Secret Agent*, MacWhirr prefers direct contact with these 'eloquent facts' to indirect contact with them through the mediation of written words. This indicates a moral strength in MacWhirr more readily than Jukes's imaginative and witty letters, and when the sea tests them both – as Conrad believed nothing else could test a man – then it is MacWhirr who most ably rises to the occasion.

When the typhoon becomes actuality rather than supposition then MacWhirr is able to use the book which previously had put him out of patience:

> [The captain], clinging to the rail, paid no attention.
> 'According to the books the worst is not over yet.'
>   'If most of them hadn't been half dead with sea-sickness and fright, not one of us would have come out of that 'tween-deck alive,' said Jukes.
>   'Had to do what's fair by them,' mumbled MacWhirr, stolidly. 'You don't find everything in books.' [T, 81]

At this testing point it is Jukes who reveals small-mindedness and an inability to escape from the particular, and MacWhirr who can conform to a generalized moral standard which leads him to behave correctly in a particular situation. *Typhoon*, then, demonstrates the same suspicion of words which do not have a 'direct relation to things and facts' as we see elsewhere in Conrad's writing, but the final weight of its moral approval is not one-sided. Books, and abstractions, are necessary, even when they don't possess an unambiguous relation to things and facts. A glimmer of hope for fiction remains.

Fiction, of all writing, can least be described as the manipulation of words which have a direct relation to things and facts. *Typhoon* is itself a work of fiction. If we are to adopt Captain MacWhirr's attitude to words, would we ever read *Typhoon*? Had Conrad adopted it, he would hardly have written the story – indeed he would not have been able to write it. Discussions of words, of language in a work of fiction cannot be innocent; they can hardly be insulated from the reader's general attitude towards the status of the work he is reading. Talking about words in a novel is akin to talking about ropes in the family of a hanged man – to borrow an example from Lord Chesterfield. So far as *Heart of Darkness* is concerned the two pieces of writing I have mentioned force the reader to consider the nature of the truth that that work of fiction is capable of revealing.

Marlow's comparison of the imperialist ventures in contemporary Africa with the Roman colonization of Britain, which occurs early on in *Heart of Darkness*, is qualified with the proviso, "if we may believe what we read'. What we believe of what we have read, and how we believe it, are questions that Conrad raises time and again for the reader, and not just in *Heart of Darkness*. Conrad himself seems constantly to have worried about the efficacy and reliability of words. Writing to his friend Cunninghame Graham on 14 January 1898, he complains:

> Half the words we use have no meaning whatever and of the other half each man understands each word after the fashion of his own folly and conceit. Faith is a myth and beliefs shift like mists on the shore; thoughts vanish; words, once pronounced, die. . . . [LCG, 65]

Conrad is far from being the most reliable commentator on his own work, and on matters both of fact and opinion he is often guilty of contradicting himself. What such passages as the above bear testimony to, I would suggest, is not necessarily Conrad's fixed opinions about the possibilities of accurate verbal communication, but more his fears concerning these possibilities. There is certainly no denying the modernist ring that this passage has: it would hardly seem out of place in a play by Pirandello or a novel by James Joyce or Virginia Woolf. Conrad certainly seems to have been prone to many of the solipsistic fears that such writers entertained (or enjoyed), and these fears are linked with worries about his skill as a writer, and even about the usefulness of writing fiction at all. In his first ever letter to Cunninghame Graham he declares:

> I am very sincerely delighted to learn that you can stand my prose. It is so hard to realize that I have any readers! – except the critics, who have been very kind and moral, and austere but excessively indulgent. To know that *You* could read me is good news indeed – for one writes only half the book; the other half is with the reader. [LCG, 46]

Now although such passages as these give convincing evidence that Conrad was, as I have said, prone to solipsistic fears such as we associate with modernism, there is, I think, a crucial difference. Conrad may worry about communicating with his readers, but in a larger philosophical sense he never doubts their existence. Nor does he ever suggest that mental processes are prior to, or independent of, an extra-mental reality. As I hope to show in a later chapter on *Nostromo*, Conrad is in the most fundamental sense a materialist rather than an idealist. But he also sees language as a very odd thing, and used to produce works of fiction he finds it bafflingly problematic.

I think that there are both personal and larger, historical, reasons for Conrad's concern with language. To touch on the latter point first, I would suggest that Conrad lived in a world dominated by *signs* to a far greater extent than ever before. Britain in Conrad's time (and we must remember that British society presumed at this time the world system of imperialism) was a society in which human relationships with other human beings and with the material world were, as never before, effected through complex systems of mediation. We need only think of the army of clerks, the growing institutionalizing of official records which so shocked Dickens, or the growth of the newspaper and publishing industries, to substantiate this point. These all constituted part of the increased power over nature that the industrial revolution ushered in by capitalism had gained for humanity, but they also had their anti-humane side to them. Whether or not such developments are *necessarily* related to capitalism or imperialism is, perhaps, open to dispute. I would however make one point which is less so.

Anonymous communication, almost unknown in primitive society, becomes more and more widespread as capitalism advances. Sending messages to an unknown person is something we all do much of the time, and yet there have been times when such events hardly occurred. Conrad often draws attention to the indirectness of the mediation between writer and reader, to the way in which messages can become detached from those who formulated them and can travel about with, as it were, an identity of their own. Such references in Conrad's novels seem to me to reflect the sort of society in which Conrad had made his home, in which many human relationships were of a curiously anonymous sort. They also reflect larger anonymities in Conrad's world – the anonymities of imperialism – as I hope shortly to demonstrate.

To give some textual substantiation to some of the points I have been arguing, I would draw attention to the various ways in which communication is pictured as a highly problematic process in *Heart of Darkness*. Think of the subtle ways in which parallels are drawn between Kurtz and Marlow in the novel, so that doubts cast on Kurtz's veracity fall too on Marlow's narrative. Both are eloquent, if in different ways, and just as we learn of Marlow from the anonymous narrator in the novel that, as darkness fell while he told his story, he 'sitting apart, had been no more to us than a voice', so too we are told that for Marlow Kurtz was no more than a voice in his own sort of darkness. The same is true, of course, of that anonymous narrator by whom Marlow's narrative is conveyed to us. Conrad's novels often portray the relationship between fictional narrator and listeners as tenuous and subject to misunderstandings, and this is surely produced by and representative of his own doubts concerning the extent to which he was able to communicate fully and accurately with his readers.

It is not hard to see why *writers* should suffer from solipsistic fears, for they are physically cut off from their readers, and their work seems to have to leave them in order to find its readers. But not all writers *have* suffered from such fears; in his book *A Common Sky*, A. D. Nuttall shows how typical of modernism solipsism is as a literary phenomenon.[4] Thus personal explanations of a writer's solipsism are, on their own, inadequate. You do not explain the overbearing sense of alienation in Kafka's novels by saying that he was a German-speaking Jew in Prague, for Kafka was able to externalize his personal experience, to find socially available symbols for his alienation, which suggests that certain forms of alienation were the rule rather than the exception in his society.

Solipsism becomes more common at a time not only when capitalism with all its inherent alienating forces is at the peak of its power, but also when the intelligentsia of countries such as Britain is increasingly isolated both from the exercise of political power and also from the process of material production. The writer who feels secure both in his or her social status and function, who can see a direct link between the activity of a writer and the larger dynamics of society, is unlikely to fall prey to solipsistic impulses. And here, I think, we can see why Conrad himself, although he is prone to solipsistic anxieties, is never overcome by them. Let us return to the two pieces of writing in *Heart of Darkness*.

Kurtz's piece of 'beautiful writing' and the *Inquiry into Some Points of Seamanship* aptly symbolize two stages of Conrad's 'duplex' life. The transition from the life of a sailor working in situations where words are used in a concrete, direct and immediate way, to sitting in front of a sheet of paper and spending perhaps hours searching for the right word, must have struck Conrad, when he meditated upon it, very forcibly. Deceitful or dishonest usages of words are soon exposed on a ship, because of the concrete nature of the tasks that have to be undertaken by collective, physical labour. Conrad refers explicitly to the contrast between the ways of life of his two careers on a number of occasions. In a humorous way he draws attention to the difference between writing 'Notices to Mariners' and novels in his essay 'Outside Literature':

> I don't mind confessing that if I were told to write a Notice to Mariners I would not pray perhaps – for I have my own convictions about the

4 A. D. Nuttall, *A Common Sky*. Sussex University Press, London, 1974.

abuse of prayer – but I would certainly fast. I would fast in the evening and get up to write my Notice to Mariners at four o'clock in the morning for fear of accidents. One letter is so soon written for another – with fatal results. [LE, 41]

One of the things about writing novels is that because there are no fatal results attendant upon the wrong letter, it is sometimes hard to say whether a mistake has or has not been made. Of his prose Conrad says in the same essay:

> yet I never learned to trust it. I can't trust it to this day. We who write prose which is not that of the Notices to Mariners are forgotten by Providence. No angel watches us at our toil. A dreadful doubt hangs over the whole achievement of literature; I mean that of its greatest and its humblest men. [LE, 43]

At the end of *Heart of Darkness* Marlow feels sure that the house will collapse and the heavens will fall on his head following his lie to Kurtz's Intended. But, as he says, the heavens do not fall for such a trifle. Heavens do not fall either when a novelist makes a mistake: where all words are fictive who is to notice particular dishonesties? Sailors may 'yarn', and may read Bulwer Lytton, but there is no room for fiction in the heart of a storm.

Marlow suggests that his listeners cannot understand what the problems which faced Kurtz were, as they are 'each moored with two good addresses ... a butcher round one corner, a policeman round another', and thus, we presume, lived in a society where restraint had been institutionalized and was no longer an individual responsibility. Setting aside the immediate significance of this remark, there is a striking paragraph in the 'Familiar Preface' to Conrad's *A Personal Record* in which he talks of the writer's need to respect truth and to take care of his own integrity:

> In that interior world where his thought and his emotions go seeking for the experience of imagined adventures, there are no policemen, no law, no pressure of circumstance or dread of opinion to keep him within bounds. Who then is going to say Nay to his temptations if not his conscience? [APR, xviii]

The writer of fiction is as much in need of personal restraint in his lawless world of the imagination as are Kurtz and Marlow in their lawless world of the Congo.

Conrad certainly seems to have felt the need for this restraint, and to have experienced how exhausting its continued operation during the writing of a novel was. In *A Personal Record* there is an extremely interesting account of Conrad's 'person from Porlock' experience of being interrupted by a visitor during the composition of *Nostromo*. Conrad stresses in this account the extent to which writing a novel seems to involve residence in another world, a world which is shattered by the greeting from 'the general's daughter' visiting his wife. This separate world is not, however, a world of comfortable retreat, but one in which Conrad's capacities are strained as much as, in different ways, they were strained by the real world of wind and sea as a sailor. The difference lies not in the effort demanded by this world of words, but in the intangibility of the rewards. The passage, although long, is worth quoting in full.

> All I know, is that, for twenty months, neglecting the common joys of life that fall to the lot of the humblest on this earth, I had, like the prophet of old, 'wrestled with the Lord' for my creation, for the head-lands of the coast, for the darkness of the Placid Gulf, the light on the snows, the clouds on the sky, and for the breath of life that had to be blown into the shapes of men and women, of Latin and Saxon, of Jew and Gentile. These are, perhaps, strong words, but it is difficult to characterize otherwise the intimacy and the strain of a creative effort in which mind and will and conscience are engaged to the full, hour after hour, day after day, away from the world, and to the exclusion of all that makes life really lovable and gentle – something for which a material parallel can only be found in the everlasting sombre stress of the westward winter passage round Cape Horn. For that too is the wrestling of men with the might of their Creator, in a great isolation from the world, without the amenities and consolations of life, a lonely struggle under a sense of over-matched littleness, for no reward that could be adequate, but for the mere winning of a longitude. Yet a certain longitude, once won, cannot be disputed. The sun and the stars and the shape of your earth are the witnesses of your gain; whereas a handful of pages, no matter how much you have made them your own, are at best but an obscure and questionable spoil. [APR, 98]

Conrad makes more or less the same point whenever he contrasts writing with physical labour: the effort is comparable, the results are not. Writing to Stephen Crane on 16 November 1897, he compares writing with breaking stones, noting that the attraction of the latter occupation is that there's no doubt about breaking a stone, while there is doubt, fear, a black horror, in every page one writes.[5]

Certainly what I earlier referred to as the 'anonymity' of communication which the solitary novelist experiences in his or her work is one of the factors which make writing such a demanding occupation. On 16 September 1899, Conrad writes to Garnett:

---

5 Carl Bohmenberger and Norman Mitchell Hill (eds), 'The Letters of Joseph Conrad to Stephen and Cora Crane'. *The Bookman* (New York), May 1929, LXIX 3, p. 230.

Even writing to a friend – to a person one has heard, touched, drank with, quarrelled with – does not give me a sense of reality. All is illusion – the words written, the mind at which they are aimed, the truth they are intended to express, the hands that will hold the paper, the eyes that will glance at the lines. Every image floats vaguely in a sea of doubt – and the doubt itself is lost in an unexplored universe of incertitudes. [LFC, 153]

Writing to Cunninghame Graham on 19 January 1900, Conrad complains that, although he has completed upwards of a hundred thousand words, 'I have lost all sense of reality; I look at the fields or sit before the blank sheet of paper as if I were in a dream' [LCG, 131].

The 'world' of writing, then, is devoid of policemen, and inspires a 'black horror' in Conrad, engendering such a sense of unreality that he feels as if he were in a dream. It sounds very like the world of the Congo into which Marlow ventures, for Marlow is not only struck by the need for restraint in the absence of law-enforcement, not only witnesses Kurtz's black horror, but also describes his own attempt to convey the reality of Kurtz to his listeners as an attempt to tell a dream:

He [Kurtz] was just a word for me. I did not see the man in the name any more than you do. Do you see him? Do you see the story? Do you see anything? It seems to me I am trying to tell you a dream – making a vain attempt, because no relation of a dream can convey the dream sensation. [HOD, 82]

The dream recurs throughout Conrad's work as the symbol of unreality or unconsciousness, and Marlow's distinction between 'relating a dream' and 'conveying the dream sensation' is one to which I wish to return. I want to draw particular attention to the statement that for Marlow Kurtz was 'just a word'. In a world dominated by signs, where human beings relate to one another through the mediation of signs rather than directly, it is not surprising that human beings should end up appearing to *be* signs rather than people. Marlow is trying to tell his listeners a dream. Conrad feels as if he is in a dream when he is writing. The connection here is not an accidental one. It is when human beings relate to one another more and more through independent signs that their resultant isolation from immediate human contact inspires the feeling that they are living a dream.

If it is the *isolation* of writing that induces a dream-like feeling of unreality for the novelist, it helps to explain why writing should itself have a symbolic force in Conrad's work. If the life that Conrad sees around him is one in which men and women are isolated from real, confirming, human contact, and deal with one another only at second hand, then their situation is in some ways comparable to that of the writer, who engages, in Vygotsky's term, in 'speech without an interlocutor' – lacking that direct contact with another individual that accompanies speech. Writing then can be seen to bear the same relation to speech as alienated existence, contact with other people at second hand through 'public selves' and impersonal signs bears to an imagined, rarely experienced, life-giving community – on board ship, for example. This helps to explain the initially puzzling fact that Conrad sometimes refers to life itself as a dream. The best known occasion is Stein's speech in *Lord Jim*, but in his introduction to Thomas Beer's study of Stephen Crane, Conrad remarks:

> Indeed, life is but a dream – especially for those of us who have never kept a diary or possessed a note-book in our lives. [LE, 93]

Life is a dream without a diary (the narrator of *The Shadow-Line*, incidentally, talks of having kept a diary twice – once in conditions of 'moral isolation'), but writing is also a dream. It seems clear that what was *not* a dream for Conrad was collective, physical work to achieve a common goal. Both life on land and the life of a writer were, in different ways, evocative of the dream state, and in his work the two serve as symbols or tokens of each other.

But the dream that Marlow is trying to tell his listeners is of Africa. Now if the life within the England of Conrad's time was unreal and dream-like, the life of imperialist exploitation of the Congo was even more so. Conrad, like many writers of his time, commented upon the alienating pressures of the contemporary city. In the same introduction to Beer's study of Crane, written only a year after Eliot had commented on the 'Unreal city' in 'The Waste Land', Conrad comments upon the streets of London, empty apart from the occasional figure, 'unreal, flitting by, obviously negligible'. In *The Secret Agent* this view of the heart of darkness of urban alienation receives its most detailed exposition by Conrad. But there is a similar passage, describing (we presume) Brussels, at the end of *Heart of Darkness*, where the distance between the narrator and those he sees in the city streets is not an 'internal' aspect of the dream-like existence of the city, but something contributed to by his experience of the imperialist exploitation of Africa initiated in that same city.

> I found myself back in the sepulchral city resenting the sight of people hurrying through the streets to filch a little money from each other, to devour their infamous cookery, to gulp their unwholesome beer, to dream their insignificant and silly dreams. They trespassed upon my thoughts. They were intruders whose knowledge of life was to me an irritating pretence, because I felt so sure they could not possibly know the things I knew. [HOD, 152]

Marlow knows so much more than those he sees in the Brussels streets: like a man returning from hell he is possessed of knowledge which makes those without it appear to be merely dreaming. Marlow has gone from the surface appearance of life through to its outer realities and ramifications in the Congo.

Without wishing to argue too mechanical or simple a relationship, I would suggest that imperialism is centrally involved in the dream-existence of people in *Heart of Darkness*, for it involves yet more extended, complex and concealed chains of mediation through signs than even life in the domestic city. And it is thus appropriate that Kurtz's report, and the distance it is from the actual 'horror', should symbolize the distance between the consciousness of those hurrying through the streets of Brussels and the horrors their labours are contributing to and indirectly controlling in the Congo. Conrad certainly seems to have seen parallels between the indirect chains of mediation between writer and reader, cut off from personal contact with each other, and the indirect chains of mediation between imperialist and exploited people. In his essay 'Henry James An Appreciation', he describes 'the creative art of a writer of fiction' in terms appropriate to a description of imperialist plunder, noting that it may be compared to

> rescue work carried out in darkness against cross gusts of wind swaying the action of a great multitude. It is rescue work, this snatching of vanishing phases of turbulence, disguised in fair words, out of the native obscurity into a light where the struggling forms may be seen, seized upon. [NLL, 13]

In his essay 'A Glance at Two Books', referring to the lack of a precise intention in the mind of the novelist writing a book, he adds:

> It never occurs to him that a book is a deed, that the writing of it is an enterprise as much as the conquest of a colony. [LE, 132]

The analogy between writing and colonial conquest would seem to rest on both the achievement of something stable, portable, permanent out of 'native obscurity', and also the indirectness of the mediation involved in both cases. Probably the most memorable picture of such a chain of indirect mediation in *Heart of Darkness* – like the writing process an essentially *non-reciprocal* one – is the early description by Marlow of the French man-of-war shelling the coast:

> There wasn't even a shed there, and she was shelling the bush. It appears the French had one of their wars going on thereabouts. Her ensign dropped limp like a rag; the muzzles of the long six-inch guns stuck out all over the low hull; the greasy, slimy swell swung her up

lazily and let her down, swaying her thin masts. In the empty im-
mensity of earth, sky, and water, there she was, incomprehensible,
firing into a continent. [HOD, 61]

The episode is obviously presented as representative of the larger
relations of imperialism – the use of coercion and brutality, but
'at a distance', cut off from their results. The French man-of-
war's crew are, like the inhabitants of Brussels, living in a dream,
isolated from the human consequences for which they are morally
responsible. The description of the French ship follows the
portrayal of a very different craft:

> Now and then a boat from the shore gave one a momentary contact
> with reality. It was paddled by black fellows. You could see from afar
> the white of their eyeballs glistening. They shouted, sang; their bodies
> streamed with perspiration; they had faces like grotesque masks – these
> chaps; but they had bone, muscle, a wild vitality, an intense energy of
> movement, that was as natural and true as the surf along their coast.
> [HOD, 61]

These Africans, surely, are finding that 'something elevating' in
physical work 'into which one puts all one's heart in association
with others and for a clearly understood purpose'. Their relations
with one another and with the physical world are all *immediate*,
unmediated by signs. The consequences of their actions are at
once apparent to them, and add to their humanity. Their
identity-confirming activity is so striking that it gives Marlow
a 'contact with reality', while the French ship is 'incomprehensible'. The French ship's flag drops 'lazily', while the Africans
have a 'wild vitality'. And the isolation of those on the man-of-
war from humanity and from reality in general is underlined by
Marlow's telling us that 'we gave her her letters (I heard the men
in that lonely ship were dying of fever at the rate of three a day).'

That indirect contact symbolized by the letter is a fitting touch
to highlight the alienated existence of those on the ship, and
the comparison with an analogous chain of indirect mediation –
writing – is further drawn attention to by referring to the ship
as 'incomprehensible'. Whereas, in the passages I quoted earlier,
writing is described in terms of colonial plundering, here colonial
war is described in terms of linguistic breakdown. The shelling
of the coast is referred to again by Marlow when he sees the
African prisoners shackled together and hears the sound of
blasting. The camp of natives being shelled by the ship contained, 'somebody on board' told Marlow, 'enemies'. The
shackled prisoners are called 'criminals'. Imperialism is not just
comparable to writing in its indirectness, it also *relies upon* the
fact that words, like shells, can be detached from their origins,

or used without heed being paid to their effects. Imperialism is the imposition of alien meanings on an unwilling recipient.

> Another report from the cliff made me think suddenly of that ship of war I had seen firing into a continent. It was the same kind of ominous voice; but these men could by no stretch of imagination be called enemies. They were called criminals, and the outraged law, like the bursting shells, had come to them, an insoluble mystery from the sea.
> [HOD, 64]

As we will see, the comparison of guns to a voice, words to shells is a favourite one of Conrad's, and it draws attention to the 'detachable' quality of the word. In his introduction to *Joseph Conrad's Letters to R. B. Cunninghame Graham*, C. T. Watts points out:

> The issue of *Blackwood's Magazine* for March 1899 contained an article called 'An Unwritten Chapter of History: the Struggle for Borgu', of which the practical efficiency of the following remarks is typical: 'The little bush-fighting that was done against Lapai and elsewhere proved the superiority of the hard bullet over that used in the Sniders. The soft bullet is apt to break up when volleys are fired into bush where natives are hiding; but the Lee-Metford projectiles went through the cover so completely that the hidden party always ran before our men could get close. . . . ' and this article accompanies the episode of 'The Heart of Darkness' in which the 'pilgrims' empty their futile rifles into the bush, and in which Kurtz scrawls 'Exterminate all the brutes!'
> [LCG, 23]

Scrawling such a phrase is not much more difficult than firing a rifle into the bush, or shelling the coast with a ship's gun. One of the things about a society or a world dominated by signs is that it is very easy to initiate unpleasant activities while remaining cut off from their realities.

Words can even be used to obscure unpleasant realities. The Chief Accountant in *Heart of Darkness* remarks that, 'when one has to make correct entries, one comes to hate those savages – hate them to the death.' Accountancy is a classic case of a profession thrown up by a society dominated by signs, by indirect human relationships mediated through marks on paper rather than direct contact. The comment recalls the early description of the Accountant who is listening to Marlow's story, who 'had brought out already a box of dominoes, and was toying architecturally with the bones'. The difference between 'making correct entries' and 'toying with bones' is not so great: in both cases things are being manipulated without regard to their living implications. A comparable example is the giving of pieces of paper signifying payment to the crew of Marlow's ship in the Congo when they are without food. The 'authorities' can content themselves with the fact that the crew were paid; that they were also starving to death is not important.

Colonialism and imperialism have in practice always seemed to demand the imposition of such inhumane order onto unwilling recipients, and it is an imposition that relies heavily on linguistic duplicity. The vocabulary of American policy in Vietnam threw up some fine examples of the genre – 'pacification', 'strategic hamlets', and so on. The horrors of colonialism and imperialism are such that those initiating the deeds have to cut themselves off from full knowledge of their nature. Keats expresses this particularly well in two stanzas from 'Isabella':

> With her two brothers this fair lady dwelt,
>   Enriched from ancestral merchandize,
> And for them many a weary hand did swelt
>   In torched mines and noisy factories,
> And many once proud-quiver'd loins did melt
>   In blood from stinging whip; – with hollow eyes
> Many all day in dazzling river stood,
> To take the rich-ored driftings of the flood.
>
> For them the Ceylon diver held his breath,
>   And went all naked to the hungry shark;
> For them his ears gush'd blood; for them in death
>   The seal on the cold ice with piteous bark
> Lay full of darts; for them alone did seethe
>   A thousand men in troubles wide and dark:
> Half-ignorant, they turn'd an easy wheel,
> That set sharp racks at work, to pinch and peel.

What is so striking about these stanzas is not so much the description of the physical pains inflicted by the brothers, though that is powerful enough; but even more acute than this is Keats's portrayal of the indirect way in which this pain is inflicted: *half-ignorant* is just right, and it applies perfectly to what we see going on in the Congo of *Heart of Darkness*. As Marlow says of the Belgians who are, we presume, staffing the home-based machinery of the Congo exploit, 'they could not possibly know the things I knew.' The troubles of those oppressed by Isabella's brothers are indeed wide and *dark*, dark because hidden from view and from full knowledge. The darkness of the Congo in *Heart of Darkness* stands for many things, but one of these is the secrecy and concealment necessary to imperialism's operation. The mechanical metaphor used by Keats – the 'easy wheel' – is also very precise. It is the industrial revolution, with its revolutionizing of production and communication, that allows human beings to inflict pain on their fellows in half-ignorance. Oppression is not new, but oppression by those hardly aware that they are oppressors is peculiarly modern.

Language is an essential part of this half-ignorance, for only human beings can abstract words from their origins in concrete experience and manipulate them independent of their origins or their eventual results. Language is both real and unreal used in this way. We can think of Kurtz's words – falsely eloquent, detached from concrete reality in one sense, but in another sense part of the reality which Marlow has to grapple with, able to bring real experience of pain and death to him. As Kurtz is crawling on all fours towards the drums and fires of the Africans, Marlow reports:

> The knitting old woman with the cat obtruded herself upon my memory as a most improper person to be sitting at the other end of such an affair. [HOD, 142]

The scene early in the novel in which Marlow meets this old woman in the European offices of the Company is heavy with symbolic overtones, and there is little doubt that she represents chance, as her portrayal makes unambiguous reference to Lachesis, one of the Fates. Marlow's comment, then, calls to mind both chance and connections – 'the other end of such an affair'. Marlow's situation at this point is both heavily dependent on chance, and also connected with what has happened in Europe.

Without arguing a direct parallel one can compare the knitting old woman with another description by Conrad of a heartless, mechanistic and indeed deterministic universe that resembles a knitting machine.

> It evolved itself (I am severely scientific) out of a chaos of scraps of iron and behold! – it knits. I am horrified at the horrible work and stand appalled. I feel it ought to embroider – but it goes on knitting. . . . And the most withering thought is that the infamous thing has made itself; made itself without thought, without conscience, without foresight, without eyes, without heart. It is a tragic accident – and it has happened. [LCG, 56]

The knitting machine described here is a perfect symbol of mechanical efficiency which inflicts pain but is impervious to the human consequences of what it does. Its operation is comparable to the work of the Chief Accountant who hates the 'savages' 'to the death', but keeps his books in apple-pie order.

Conrad's 'infamous knitting machine' reminds me of works in many ways very different – Blake's 'The Tyger' and Mary Shelley's *Frankenstein* – which both associate images of machinery and industrialism with creations which 'go wrong', and which end up oppressing the creator. It is not accidental that these works should be written at a time when emergent capitalism is developing both the forces of production and also the sum of human misery and exploitation. As Marx puts it in *Capital*:

> within the capitalist system all methods for raising the social pro-
> ductiveness of labour are brought about at the cost of the individual
> labourer; all means for the development of production transform them-
> selves into means of domination over, and exploitation of, the pro-
> ducers; they mutilate the labourer into a fragment of a man, degrade
> him to the level of an appendage of a machine, destroy every remnant
> of charm in his work and turn it into a hated toil; they estrange from
> him the intellectual potentialities of the labour-process in the same
> proportion as science is incorporated in it as an independent power.[6]

Conrad's knitting machine, Blake's tiger and Mary Shelley's monster are all related to the basic process so graphically described by Marx. The last phrase in the above quotation may help us to understand Conrad's remark about being 'strictly scientific'. Conrad's dislike of science is based on his perception of the appropriation of science by capitalism as an independent power to oppress humanity, although it should be said that his perception is a partial one and that these are not the terms that he would have used.

In *Heart of Darkness*, then, Marlow has the job of dissipating the half-ignorance of his listeners, informing them of the nature of his experiences in Africa. But this involves certain difficulties. If the experiential reality of the heart of darkness is what the European conceals from his conscious knowledge, how can this felt experience be conveyed to his listeners? If Marlow's experi-ence was 'inexpressible', as he says it was, then how can it be given to them or to us? These questions are closely intertwined in *Heart of Darkness* with questions about how a writer manages to convey the truth of his own 'dream' to his far-distant readers. Marlow's solution is an interesting one, and it applies to both situations I have outlined:

> 'No, it is impossible; it is impossible to convey the life-sensation of
> any given epoch of one's existence – that which makes its truth, its
> meaning – its subtle and penetrating essence. It is impossible. We live,
> as we dream – alone. . . .'
> He paused again as if reflecting, then added –
> 'Of course in this you fellows see more than I could then. You see
> me, whom you know.' [HOD, 82]

At first glance, the passage seems contradictory. Marlow starts off by saying that he cannot convey the lived experience of an epoch of his life, then moves on to concede that his listeners see

6 Karl Marx, *Capital* I. Lawrence and Wishart, London, 1967, p. 645.

more than he could then. What I think is happening here is that Marlow, unable to express the 'inexpressible', is able to express its inexpressibility. And his listeners, although they do not *experience* the life sensation of Marlow's heart of darkness, *understand* what it is that has happened to him. This distinction between experience and understanding is rather an important one, and can perhaps be expanded by picking up Marlow's suggestion that experience is like a dream. We cannot get someone actually to experience the sensation of a dream that we have had, but we can tell them about it. Indeed, we only *understand* a dream by being in some way detached from our experience of it, by separating ourselves from it and looking at it 'from outside'.[7] In doing this we are exercising that peculiarly human capacity to separate ourselves from our past and present experiences in order better to understand them.

This distinction between experience and knowledge is one that Conrad makes in different ways very frequently in his work. His habit of burying narrative within narrative in his novels – and *Heart of Darkness* is a good example of this – is a way of enacting this objectification of experience. The narrator does not experience, he or she recounts and comments on an experience. Indeed there is internal evidence in *Heart of Darkness* that Conrad saw meaning to be separate from experience:

> To [Marlow] the meaning of an episode was not inside like a kernel but outside, enveloping the tale which brought it out only as a glow brings out a haze, in the likeness of one of these misty halos that sometimes are made visible by the spectral illumination of moonshine. [HOD, 48]

The comment could be taken as a comment both on imperialism, the meaning of which cannot be found in the experience of actual exploitation, and also on human experience in general, which is understood to the extent that it is surveyed in a wider context than in terms of its immediate life sensation. The distinction is, I think, a revolutionary insight of Conrad's, and it strikes me as cruelly appropriate that E. M. Forster – who would be the arch-priest of liberal humanists were liberal humanists to allow themselves arch-priests – delivered the famous criticism of Conrad that 'the secret casket of his genius contains a vapour rather than a jewel',[8] situating truth *inside*, in the kernel, within

7 Sigmund Freud, in *The Interpretation of Dreams*, notes that 'in dreams – as a rule ... – we appear not to *think* but to *experience*; that is to say, we attach complete belief to the hallucinations. Not until we wake up does the critical comment arise that we have not experienced anything but have merely been thinking in a particular way, or in other words dreaming.' (Pelican edn, Harmondsworth, 1976, p. 115).

8 E. M. Forster, 'Joseph Conrad: a Note'. Reprinted in *Abinger Harvest*, Penguin, Harmondsworth, 1967, p. 152.

the casket, or come to that, hidden in the Marabar caves, rather than in the knitting room of Brussels or in Marlow's account of his experiences, displaced from, not contained in, the actual sensation.

To turn from imperialism to Conrad's account of it in *Heart of Darkness*, I would argue that just as Marlow tells his listeners that they could 'see more' than he could, so too the readers of the novel, looking at Marlow through the eyes of the primary narrator of the text, far from being cut off from the events described, are in a better position fully to understand them precisely because the narrative is displaced from them. We understand aspects of imperialism better by seeing Marlow's incomprehension of them, or inability to describe them, than we would by actually having these experiences sensuously evoked for us. Why? Because a central constituent of imperialism is the half-ignorance of the imperialist, and we cannot, logically, *see* ignorance by *being* ignorant. Wittgenstein points out that one does not possess the concept of negative number by being in debt,[9] and this is a distinction that is often forgotten. One of the unquestioned assumptions often made by literary critics is that the greatest literature evokes experiences in the reader; it is arguable that if it only does this then it does not do enough, for literature should help us to understand as well as to experience. If we bear in mind Marlow's comment that 'you fellows see more than I could then', and if I am correct to argue that the verb 'to see' here is meant to be distinguished from 'conveying the life-sensation', then Conrad's famous words in the preface to *The Nigger of the 'Narcissus'* assume an important significance:

> My task which I am trying to achieve is, by the power of the written word to make you hear, to make you feel – it is, before all, to make you *see*. [NON, xxvi]

If this is insufficiently explicit Conrad continues a few lines further on from this in words remarkably similar to those of Marlow's which I have just quoted.

> To snatch in a moment of courage, from the remorseless rush of time, a passing phase of life, is only the beginning of the task. The task approached in tenderness and faith is to hold up unquestioningly, without choice and without fear, the rescued fragment before all eyes in the light of a sincere mood. [NON, xxvi]

The passage is a difficult one, but the fundamental distinction between 'snatching a phase of life' and 'holding it up before all eyes' seems to resemble Marlow's distinction between 'conveying the life-sensation' and giving an episode meaning.

9 L. Wittgenstein, *Zettel*. Blackwell, Oxford, 1967, p. 61.

As I have already suggested, this sort of distinction involves important questions about what literature is, and also about how literature achieves its ends. David Thorburn, in his perceptive book *Conrad's Romanticism*, argues that what Dr Leavis refers to as the 'adjectival insistence' in *Heart of Darkness* and *Lord Jim* is an essential part of their meaning.[10] It is Marlow's inability to convey certain feelings which is testified to by such 'adjectival insistence', and in this way both novels manage to tell us something over and above the experiences of their participating characters. Like Marlow's listeners in *Heart of Darkness*, we 'fellows see more than I could then.' Dr Leavis associates Marlow's incoherence with a failure of meaning in the book, whereas it is a part of that book's meaning.

By *talking about* his Congo experiences Marlow proceeds from inarticulate experience to coherent understanding. Kurtz must move in the opposite direction, from articulate misrepresentation of the realities of imperialism to semi-articulate experience of them. The scrawled note, 'Exterminate all the brutes', and the hardly coherent gasp, 'The horror! The horror!', give evidence of Kurtz's final achieved contact with the realities undreamed of in his beautiful writing. Marlow and Kurtz thus can be taken as polar opposites: Marlow is adjectivally insistent, but aware of certain experiential realities; Kurtz is 'eloquent' but ignorant of these same realities. In the course of the novel both move towards each other to a certain achieved balance of experience and knowledge, a certain identity which Marlow recognizes and respects in his view of Kurtz's 'summing up'.

> It was an affirmation, a moral victory paid for by innumerable defeats, by abominable terrors, by abominable satisfactions. But it was a victory!
> [HOD, 151]

There is so much evidence of Conrad's extremely scrupulous attitude towards language that the suggestion that he was unaware of the inadequacy of Marlow's adjectives is unconvincing. For example, writing to Sir Hugh Clifford the year after *Heart of Darkness* was published, he commented on a piece of Clifford's writing as follows:

> You do not leave enough to the imagination. I do not mean as to facts – the facts cannot be too explicitly stated; I am alluding simply to the phrasing. True, a man who knows so much ... may well spare himself the trouble of meditating over the words, only that words, groups of words, ... have the power in their sound or their aspect to present the very thing you wish to hold up before the mental vision of your readers.

10 David Thorburn, *Conrad's Romanticism*. Yale University Press, New Haven and London, 1974, p. 117.

The things 'as they are' exist in words; therefore words should be handled with care lest the picture, the image of truth abiding in facts, should become distorted – or blurred. [JCLL I, 279]

Conrad's advice is followed by an extremely sensitive piece of verbal criticism, analysing a passage of Clifford's. At one point in this Conrad comments: 'No word is adequate. The imagination of the reader should be left free to arouse his feeling.' The point has implications for Conrad's own prose style. It suggests that we should not assume that Conrad set himself the task of arousing 'concrete particularities' of sensation in the reader. The New Critical orthodoxy – now a little battered – is that literature should use the precise word to evoke a precise and particular response in the reader. Conrad's advice to Clifford runs counter to this orthodoxy, suggesting that at certain times at any rate words should be left out, or words should be used in such a way as to draw attention to their own inadequacy. Just as we are to *look at* Marlow's experiences rather than to *experience* them, so too there may be occasions where Conrad wants us to look at words, rather than to experience sensations through them. I have in mind here the sort of distinction a linguistician makes between 'opaque' and 'transparent' words. There is a very powerful section in Conrad's essay 'The Crime of Partition' in which he follows his own advice strikingly. Discussing those who have died, 'East and West', in the war, he writes:

[They] died neither for democracy, nor leagues, nor systems, nor yet for abstract justice, which is an unfathomable mystery. *They died for something too deep for words*, too mighty for the common standards by which reason measures the advantages of life and death, too sacred for the vain discourses that come and go on the lips of dreamers, fanatics, humanitarians, and statesmen. They died. . . . [NLL, 128]

The emphasis is mine, but the final ellipsis is Conrad's. Where something is too deep for words then you leave words out. The passage thus enacts its own message by passing over in silence that about which Conrad feels we cannot speak. It is not too outrageous to suggest that Conrad is using a comparable technique in his 'adjectival insistence'.

Conrad, in a well known comment on his trip to the Congo in 'Geography and Some Explorers', says that the trip left no great haunting memory,

but only the unholy recollection of a prosaic newspaper 'stunt' and the distasteful knowledge of the vilest scramble for loot that ever disfigured the history of human conscience and geographical exploration. What an end to the idealized realities of a boy's daydreams! [LE, 17]

Kurtz too is initially an idealist, with his plans for spreading light in Africa. Marlow tells us early on in the novel that he never imagined Kurtz as doing, but as discoursing, and this separation of speech from activity, from work, is significant. Indeed, Marlow discovers later on that you don't even discourse with Kurtz, you listen to him. As we will see most clearly in *Under Western Eyes*, Conrad appears to hold that the more language is used in the presence of other people and directed towards a common task then the more reliable it is. The novelist writes in isolation, and his words are not directly connected to any concrete task: we listen to him discourse as Marlow listened to Kurtz. It thus behoves us to be as suspicious of his words as Marlow is of Kurtz's, to ensure that they do not just constitute beautiful writing which bears no relationship to actuality.

Conrad made it clear that the final scene in the novel between Marlow and Kurtz's Intended was crucial to its meaning. The very name of the Intended is ironic, of course, for Kurtz is characterized by unimplemented intentions and unfulfilled ideals. Writing to David Meldrum on 2 January 1899, Conrad noted that 'a mere shadow of love interest [is present] just in the last pages – but I hope that it will have the effect I intend', and the suggestion seems to be that an element of sexual attraction is present between Marlow and the Intended, much as we catch brief glimpses of a similar, unacknowledged attraction between the narrator of *Under Western Eyes* and Nathalie Haldin. Three years after writing the above comment to Meldrum, Conrad penned the following lines to William Blackwood, referring to

> the last pages of Heart of Darkness where the interview of the man and the girl locks in – as it were – the whole 30000 words of narrative description into one suggestive view of a whole phase of life, and makes of that story something quite on another plane than an anecdote of a man who went mad in the Centre of Africa. [LBM, 154]

What is the 'locking in' of which Conrad speaks? What is it that this final scene conveys that raises the rest of the narrative onto 'another plane'? The scene is perhaps the most powerful and evocative in all Conrad's work, and the roots of its effectiveness are extraordinarily complex, but what seems to me to be dominant in the scene is the isolation of the Intended from the real world; her idealism puts her out of touch with reality, puts her beyond human contact. Marlow cannot – does not want to – get through to her. What is I think important is that this isolation is presented in a very ambivalent way: Marlow is first angry with her, then softens in his attitude. She is out of touch with reality, yet perhaps she represents the need for unreal ideals that human beings are possessed of. Marlow's comments on his aunt's idealism at the start of the novel may perhaps serve as a commentary on the Intended, and may suggest that Conrad saw the Intended not as a unique individual, but as representative of something more fundamental:

> 'It's queer how out of touch with truth women are. They live in a world of their own, and there had never been anything like it, and never can be. It is too beautiful altogether, and if they were to set it up it would go to pieces before the first sunset.' [HOD, 59]

The comment follows his aunt's unrealistic comments on '"weaning those ignorant millions from their horrid ways"', echoing the 'rot let loose in print and talk at that time', and the 'world of their own' in which women live in *Heart of Darkness* is in both the cases of Marlow's aunt and the Intended associated with imperialism. One way in which the final scene can be taken as a 'locking in' of the whole book is by interpreting it as the final 'knitting in' to the complicities of imperialism of Marlow himself. Marlow cannot tell the Intended the truth. He recognizes that it would be 'too dark altogether'. Imperialism demands that sections of the domestic power retain their illusions, and thus the human relationships of that domestic power are impregnated by the lies of imperialism through and through.

Kurtz tries to set up that 'too beautiful' world, but instead of weaning ignorant savages there is a strong suggestion that they wean him on to the eating of human flesh: we are told that the heads on the stockade are food for thought, and there are frequent references in *Heart of Darkness* to eating which have a cannibalistic flavour to them. It is important to Marlow that the Intended should not become acquainted with 'the horror', however, and the relationship between Marlow and the Intended duplicates that between Kurtz and her: Marlow is forced to reproduce her illusions for her, and thus to take part in reproducing the half-ignorance upon which imperialism thrives.

The Intended represents the human capacity for imaginative illusions, for escaping from the concrete. As I have suggested, this capacity carries with it both power and vulnerabilities. Imperialism as a process illustrates this perfectly, providing a complex stimulus to the domestic powers to increase human control over nature while making them subject to illusions about what they are doing. The scene explicitly associates these illusions with language: the sound of the Intended's voice seems to Marlow to have the accompaniment of all the other sounds we have, throughout the novel, associated with 'the horror'. Her voice *is* a part of that horror, just as the knitting woman is connected with Kurtz.

Marlow's comments on the Intended should not be taken as representative of Conrad's views on women in general. Antonia Avellanos in *Nostromo* and Winnie in *The Secret Agent* are no less realists, in the common sense of the word, than are other male characters in these novels. Abstracting a general picture of Conrad's view of women from his novels is no simple task, and where Conrad seems to be generalizing (as, for instance, in *Heart of Darkness* or in *Chance*), his comments are sometimes indicative of the limitations of Marlow's attitudes. An instructive parallel can be drawn with Conrad's views on race. It is possible to abstract certain comments from his novels and letters which suggest a rather simple-minded racial prejudice on Conrad's part, but this is only (in general) if their literary context is ignored. The narrative qualification of Razumov's anti-semitic remark in *Under Western Eyes* [UWE, 287], and Conrad's 'Author's Note' to *Almayer's Folly*, as well as the portrayal of Hirsch in *Nostromo* and Conrad's disavowal of such prejudice elsewhere in his letters[11] have to be set against such an attri-bution of attitudes to Conrad.

Similarly, there is evidence that Conrad had no simple, unqualified attitude towards 'women in general'. In *Nostromo* Decoud writes to his sister:

> The women of our country are worth looking at during a revolution. The rouge and pearl powder fall off, together with that passive attitude towards the outer world which education, tradition, custom impose upon them from the earliest infancy. [N, 234]

Conrad was certainly aware of – if not in support of – the view that women, like men, were at least in part the product of their circumstances.

The Intended's circumstances are those of the woman left behind in Europe while her fiance travels to the Congo. Perry Anderson, in his essay 'Components of the National Culture', has argued that British anthropology has a higher status than other academic disciplines because during the imperialist period scientific study of subject peoples was more acceptable than scientific study of domestic society.

> The British bourgeoisie had learnt to fear the meaning of 'general ideas' during the French Revolution: after Burke, it never forgot the lesson. Hegemony at home demanded a moratorium on them. By the end of the nineteenth century, however, this class was master of a third of the world. English anthropology was born of this disjuncture.

---

11 See, for instance, his comments to Galsworthy on a review which implies that he is Jewish, quoted by Norman Sherry in *Conrad: The Critical Heritage*, p. 231.

British imperial society exported its totalizations on its subject peoples. There, and there only, it could afford scientific study of the social whole.[12]

But it could not afford such study of the larger whole – the relationship between the imperial society and the subject peoples. The truth that is experienced in Africa cannot be told to the Intended. It is for this reason that Marlow is, in Eliot's phrase, 'unable to say a word' to the Intended.

If, as Conrad suggests, the writing of a book is like the conquest of a colony, it is perhaps in the separation of the words in the book from the reality which gives rise to them and the reality which in part they create. I have already quoted Conrad's letter to Garnett in which he talks of the gap between a letter and personal contact with a friend. It is the portability of words, their ability to rise above concrete circumstances, that gives them their power and their vulnerability. Kurtz's words, as Marlow reassures the Intended, will remain. Kurtz's Congo experiences will die with Marlow. Kurtz, for the Intended, *is* his words. There is a strong suggestion that Conrad was similarly aware of a gap between his own, fictional words and the life which gave rise to them. In the letter to Garnett Conrad wrote as if the experience was the reality and the written words an illusion (a paradox, it is worth noting, because the distinction is made *in* a letter to Garnett, which is a letter commenting on the unreliability and unreality of letters!). Elsewhere he makes a similar distinction between 'concrete experience' and 'written words' of a sort that recalls the distinction between the horror of the Congo and the beautiful writing of Kurtz, but reverses the value judgement. In his book *Joseph Conrad's Mind and Method*, R. L. Mégroz quotes from a letter he received from Conrad:

> A man expressing himself in imaginative literature can never really be worth more than what he gives to the world: his, as it were, disembodied personality; for the simple reason that the flesh is weak (as has been observed before) and moreover may be encumbered by unlovely and even contemptible material characteristics. The thought also as formulated in speech may be affected by the passing little incidents of the day, and cannot have the value either in truth or sincerity of the meditated page.[13]

The contrast between this comment and Conrad's earlier opinion expressed in the letter to Garnett exposes a problem which

---

12 Perry Anderson, 'Components of the National Culture'. In Alexander Cockburn and Robin Blackburn (eds), *Student Power*, Penguin, London, reprinted 1970, p. 264.

13 R. L. Mégroz, *Joseph Conrad's Mind and Method: a Study of Personality in Art*. Faber, London, 1931, p. 23.

Heart of Darkness relentlessly explores: if words are able to rise above 'life-sensations', then where does truth reside, in the words, or in the experience they describe? The novel, unlike the comments in the two letters, does not present us with a simple answer. Words can tell lies, but they can tell truths beyond any that can exist in unverbalized sensations.

2

Lord Jim: facts and ideas

The opening words of Conrad's first published novel, *Almayer's Folly*, sum up a central element in his work in general, and in *Lord Jim* in particular:

> 'Kaspar! Makan!'
> The well-known shrill voice startled Almayer from his dream of splendid future into the unpleasant realities of the present hour. [AF, 3]

Dreams of splendid future and unpleasant realities of the present hour: the alternatives are very similar to those which face Jim throughout the novel. In addition, it is not just a contrast between these alternatives in the abstract that Conrad gives us in the above opening or in *Lord Jim*, for they are set in the precise situation of the European colonist. The dreams are those of the colonist abroad, and they are shattered by the pressures of the real and the immediate that are forced upon him by 'his' subject people. In one sense *Lord Jim* can be seen to continue the theme of idealism destroyed that we see in *Heart of Darkness*. The title of the novel picks up that strange dual identity forced upon the colonist – a Lord to 'natives', but, as the familiar term following suggests, not a 'real' Lord. The division in Jim's character is not associated so neatly with travel to a colony as is Kurtz's loss of ideals; imperialism certainly is involved in the contrast between Jim's dreams of splendid future and unpleasant realities, but in a more diffuse, deep-rooted, ideological sense than in Kurtz's case. Indeed, we are first introduced to this tension between immediate facts and ideas in Jim's life in a scene which occurs before he has ever left England. Learning the craft of the sea in an officers' training ship in England, Jim finds it hard to address himself to the demands of immediate, concrete reality:

> On the lower deck in the babel of two hundred voices he would forget himself, and beforehand live in his mind the sea-life of light literature. He saw himself saving people from sinking ships, cutting away masts in a hurricane, swimming through a surf with a line; or as a lonely castaway, barefooted and half naked, walking on uncovered

reefs in search of shellfish to stave off starvation. He confronted savages
on tropical shores, quelled mutinies on the high seas, and in a small
boat upon the ocean kept up the hearts of despairing men – always
an example of devotion to duty, and as unflinching as a hero in a book.
   'Something's up. Come along.'
   He leaped to his feet. The boys were streaming up the ladders. Above
could be heard a great scurrying about and shouting, and when he
got through the hatchway he stood still – as if confounded. [LJ, 5]

'Forgetting himself' and 'beforehand living in his mind' disastrous events are what contribute to Jim's fatal jump. His
predisposition to dream, to separate himself from the life sur-
rounding him, makes him vulnerable to error. But this is no
innate fatal flaw. As I have suggested, it cannot be understood
without at least some reference to the various forms of escape
implicit in the workings of imperialism.

   In support of this contention I would draw attention to the
substance of Jim's dreams. Saving people from sinking ships,
confronting savages on tropical shores, quelling mutinies on the
high seas – all these are activities connected with Britain's
imperial position. Jim's dreams are fuelled by 'the sea-life of light
literature', by the literary reflection of Britain's world political
role. Jim may not have set foot outside England, but his imagination has been fuelled by books: he even imagines himself 'as
unflinching as a hero in a book'. The passage quoted above
associates that escape from concrete reality that is involved in
dreams of empire with the reading of light fiction. Both represent
different ways in which Jim's contemporaries were able to escape
from unpleasant realities into dreams of splendid future – by
going abroad, or by reading a book.

   I suggested in my previous chapter that a use – or misuse –
of the power of language to escape from the here and now while
maintaining a controlling influence over it through complex
chains of mediation, was radically involved in the operation of
imperialism. *Lord Jim* seems to me to extend this analysis of the
relationship and analogies between indirect political control and
that indirect power over facts provided by language. And in
Lord Jim, I think, Conrad starts to ask more direct questions
about the particular usage of words that is fiction, about the
extent to which the reading of fiction is a means of achieving
knowledge of and control over reality – or of escaping from it.
'Controlling' and 'escaping from' appear to be very different
things. But they are closely related, for we have to a certain extent
to distance ourselves from that which we want to control, and thin
partitions divide the bounds of controlling and escaping from
reality. Jim's problem throughout the novel is his inability to

control his dreams: properly controlled they would help him to regulate his life imaginatively, out of control they destroy it.

What renders Jim incapable of controlling his dreams is not just a personal defect, but the pressure of a national ability to escape from the unpleasant realities of the present hour by participation in imperialist ventures. Even in his naval officer's school – the place in which, we know from his 'Memorandum', Conrad considered boys could most effectively learn the 'sailor mentality' – Jim is waylaid by 'the sea-life of light literature'. He prefers the anonymous voice of an author to 'the babel of two hundred voices', a voice that offers him the personal equivalent of that national escape for which he is being trained. In addition to his 'Memorandum', there is further evidence that Conrad had a very high opinion of the formative influence on a boy of a naval education: J. H. Retinger, in his book *Conrad and his Contemporaries*, writes:

> Although Borys [Conrad's son] was not showing any inclination or aptitude for the sailoring profession, nor had his father ever thought about such a career for his son, he considered that a naval school is the best for any boy, because it prepares him for practical emergencies, gives a lot of physical training, and develops mental agility by the extensive teaching of mathematics, which Conrad thought equipped one better for general thinking than dead languages or philosophical dialectics.[1]

The comment is useful evidence that Conrad saw that both an ability to deal with immediate, practical problems and also 'mental agility' and 'general thinking' were a necessary part of a satisfactory education. Conrad is no simple empiricist. But Jim's failure in life after having had such an education raises questions about the dangers of an education which excludes philosophical dialectics; for Conrad, as the passage I have already quoted from *Lord Jim* suggests, it raised questions about the general thinking associated with the reading of fiction and dreaming about empire.

Paul Kirschner, in his *Conrad: The Psychologist as Artist*, writes of Jukes, in *Typhoon*, that he

> is more vulnerable to the typhoon than MacWhirr because his imagination colours facts with larger significance, and because his intelligence, made to control events and unable to do so, logically concludes the impossibility of survival.[2]

Much the same is true of Conrad's earlier creation, Jim, although Jim does have the ability to rise to some practical emergencies,

1 J. H. Retinger, *Conrad and his Contemporaries*. Minerva, London, 1941, p. 113. [I have altered Retinger's 'Boris' to 'Borys'].
2 Paul Kirschner, *Conrad: the Psychologist as Artist*. Oliver and Boyd, Edinburgh, 1968, p. 113.

as we will see. Jim's failure is a failure to relate the concrete and
the abstract: in the course of the novel he oscillates between
extremes of near total idealism and an inability to escape from
brute facts at all. In this respect he resembles not Jukes, but
Kurtz.

Jim's polar inadequacies are both involved in and summed up
by his changing attitude to language. At the start of the novel
the words of the light literature he reads are more real to him
than the practical emergency taking place around him; by the
end of the novel he makes no distinction between words and that
to which they refer – including, most significantly, his own name.
It is as if, warned off the treachery of 'general ideas' and specula-
tive words, he wants to attach every word to a particular piece of
reality.

Marlow, we may remember from *Heart of Darkness*, admired
the manual of seamanship for its concern with the right way of
going to work. Immediately after the passage from *Lord Jim* that
I have quoted above, when Jim has missed the chance to take
part in a real emergency, we learn that he

> felt angry with the brutal tumult of earth and sky for taking him un-
> awares and checking unfairly a generous readiness for narrow escapes.
> Otherwise he was rather glad he had not gone into the cutter, since
> a lower achievement had served the turn. He had enlarged his knowl-
> edge more than those who had done the work. [LJ, 7]

For Conrad, I suspect, knowledge was never enlarged without
work, and it is an important, although often neglected, element
in Jim's subsequent career that he is placed in a situation where
work is easy to avoid. For all the real class divisions on board
ship, it is fair to say that work, particularly physical work, was
the lot of all crew members. Conrad's attitude to colonialism is
conditioned by the way it allows of a separation of mental and
physical labour, the latter being done by 'natives' rather than
white men. When Jim is in hospital, before his fatal leap, he
meets with various white men who had been thrown into the
port by accident and had not moved on.

> They had now a horror of the home service, with its harder conditions,
> severer view of duty, and the hazard of stormy oceans.... They
> shuddered at the thought of hard work, and led precariously easy
> lives. [LJ, 10]

This corrupting influence is one to which Jim is especially
vulnerable: we have learned early on that

> He knew the magic monotony of existence between sky and water:
> he had to bear the criticism of men, the exactions of the sea, and the

prosaic severity of the daily task that gives bread – but whose only reward is in the perfect love of the work. This reward eluded him. [LJ, 8]

Jim's individual propensity to idle dreams, already ideologically nurtured by imperialism, is offered fertile soil in a land occupied by work-shy white men and exploited natives. Conrad's account of Jim's anger at the brutal tumult of the earth and sky which had 'unfairly [checked] a generous readiness for narrow escapes' has a Swiftean contempt in it for Jim's powers of self-deception. But Jim finds a world in which this self-deception will be less seriously challenged by events, and the historical and political location of Jim's weakness are important to a full understanding of its development. The expatriate white men, in whose actions, looks and persons could be detected 'the soft spot, the place of decay, the determination to lounge safely through existence', are connected with the hallucinations of the engineer who sees the millions of pink toads. Jim does not see pink toads, but he sees a ship sink which remains afloat. It is white men, not 'natives', who suffer from illusions in *Lord Jim*.

As in *Heart of Darkness* a key word in *Lord Jim* is 'idea'. Imagining valorous deeds, Jim is 'so pleased with the idea that he smiled', while at the enquiry he is, in contrast, cast down by the insistent demand for facts. The facts of the sea which MacWhirr found eloquent (unusually, Conrad does not seem to have been using the word 'eloquent' in a pejorative sense here) are seen in a very different way by Jim:

They wanted facts. Facts! They demanded facts from him, as if facts could explain anything! [LJ, 21]

Jim's understanding of the relationship between facts and ideas at this point is utterly confused. Rather than appreciating that it is because he lives in a world of private fantasies that he is cut off from other men, he sees a

serried circle of facts that had surged up all about him to cut him off from the rest of his kind. [LJ, 23]

Marlow sees ideas, rather than facts to be at the heart of Jim's difficulties. As H. M. Daleski puts it, Jim shows that he is not a coward, so the source of his failure has to be sought elsewhere, and Daleski suggests that Jim is disabled by the liveliness of his imagination.[3] Marlow has a complex view of the world of facts and the world of ideas which is explicitly related to the English background which he and Jim share. Much is made of the fact that Jim is 'one of us'. The phrase assumes various meanings

3 H. M. Daleski, *Joseph Conrad: the Way of Dispossession*, Faber, London, 1977, p. 88.

in *Lord Jim*, but there is no doubt that one of these is the solidarity of the colonialists – a meaning made explicit towards the end of the novel when Marlow comments of Dain Waris that although brave and intelligent and able to fight after the manner of white men,

> He had not Jim's racial prestige and the reputation of invincible, supernatural power. He was not the visible, tangible incarnation of unfailing truth and of unfailing victory. Beloved, trusted, and admired as he was, he was still one of *them*, while Jim was one of *us*. [LJ, 266]

Marlow's concern with Jim is (like Brierly's) coloured with this feeling of racial and ideological solidarity; he is interested in Jim's affair because Jim is 'one of us' and because he came from

> the right place; he was one of us. He stood there for all the parentage of his kind, for men and women by no means clever or amusing, but whose very existence is based upon honest faith, and upon the instinct of courage. [LJ, 32]

'Faith' is a key term for Marlow: he sees Jim and his kind to be

> backed by a faith invulnerable to the strength of facts, to the contagion of example, to the solicitation of ideas. Hang ideas! They are tramps, vagabonds, knocking at the back-door of your mind, each taking a little of your substance, each carrying away some crumb of that belief in a few simple notions you must cling to if you want to live decently and would like to die easy! [LJ, 32]

I find this an extraordinary passage. 'Faith', 'a few simple notions', are counterposed both to 'facts' and 'ideas'. The comment perceptively notes the ideological threat to imperialism posed both by facts and by ideas. Imperialism relied on an ability to escape from the concrete, an ability effectively to manipulate the physical world and some of its inhabitants, by the development of productive forces not possible without that displacement from the immediate afforded by language and intellectual effort. But that same displacement also threatened imperialism: having been rather slighting about E. M. Forster in the previous chapter, I must acknowledge his achievement in *A Passage to India*, a novel which reveals how deeply embedded in the colonial mentality was a horror of intellectualism. Marlow's 'faith' incorporates that 'half-ignorant' use of ideas to control facts which did not allow the raising of awkward questions. Imperialism, like capitalism, needs an accurate knowledge of nature, but cannot afford such a knowledge of itself.

Early on in the novel Conrad makes the limits of that faith of 'all the parentage of his kind' quite explicit. Jim comes originally from a parsonage, and

Jim's father possessed such certain knowledge of the Unknowable as made for the righteousness of people in cottages without disturbing the ease of mind of those whom an unerring Providence enables to live in mansions. [LJ, 4]

It is here, indeed, that he engages in the course of 'light holiday literature' that arouses his interest in the sea. There seems little doubt that Conrad had a very shrewd idea of the reason why the faith described by Marlow should have arisen in the form it assumed. Conrad is, admittedly, far more ironical in his description of Jim's father's 'knowledge of the Unknowable' than in the latter description by Marlow of the 'faith invulnerable to the strength of facts'. But the earlier passage sets Marlow's less critical attitude in a sharper light; Marlow may approve unreservedly of this faith, but it is hard to believe that Conrad expects the reader so to do.

Marlow's description of ideas as tramps and vagabonds brings together a petty-bourgeois horror of beggars and suspicion of the intellect. Like tramps, ideas have no fixed home; they wander from place to place appearing to feed off established realities. It is oddly fitting that Jim's final downfall should be brought about by the maritime tramp Gentleman Brown.[4]

The 'few simple notions' which must be clung to in order to live 'decently' are such as to allow one to rise above immediate experiences, to become more than just a succession of unrelated day-to-day sensations. They are also, however, a safeguard against knowing too much. Jim is seen to lack this faith, and so he neither dies easily nor lives decently. Seeing too much, allowing his imagination too free a play, leads to his fatal jump. But reacting against this experience he becomes too rooted in simple facts. Had he had less imagination he would never have jumped; had he had a little more he would not have brought about his own death.

The change in Jim is brought about by the loss of a name, and it is instructive to see how a loss of 'just the name' has a similar effect on Brierly, who also kills himself as a result:

> 'Hang it, we must preserve professional decency or we become no better than so many tinkers going about loose. We are trusted. Do you understand? – trusted! Frankly, I don't care a snap for all the pilgrims that ever came out of Asia, but a decent man would not have behaved like this to a full cargo of old rags in bales. We aren't an organized body of men, and the only thing that holds us together is just the name for that kind of decency. Such an affair destroys one's confidence. A man may go pretty near through his whole sea-life without any call to show a stiff upper lip. But when the call comes . . . Aha! . . . If I . . . .' [LJ, 50]

4 I am indebted to Terry Eagleton for this point.

Jim too feels that he is trusted, and that he betrays his trust. The feeling that those of a different race have shown more solidarity (Brierly is unable to face the fact that the two Lascar seamen stuck to their posts), destroys the confidence of both Jim and of Brierly: without a 'name' they both perish. Brierly's 'tinker' is comparable with Marlow's 'tramps, vagabonds'; rather than become one himself, he kills himself. Brierly is, it should be said, talking of British sailors, not of the British as a race or as colonists. But this narrower grouping is involved in the wider one: the Malay at the enquiry who cannot believe that the white men left the ship through fear of death is not just exhibiting an attitude towards British sailors.

Jim's initial tragedy is that he chooses to expose his dreams to the very reality most likely to destroy them. Brought up on the sea-life of light literature, he finds that

> In no other life [but the sea is the illusion more wide of the] reality – in no other is the beginning *all* illusion – the disenchantment more swift – the subjugation more complete. [LJ, 94]

Perhaps it is precisely because the reality of a sea-life offers the possibility of escaping from one set of unpleasant realities that it gives rise to an escapist literature which conceals its own set of unpleasant realities. 'The sea' is a topic bound up very intimately with British imperialism: it secured Britain's borders and was a hard fact for rivals to face, but it was also the glamorous escape from the everyday realities from which wealth could be gained, and thus could become the dream of boys throughout the land. Because it was such an important fact it was transformed into a dominating idea. But the contrast between fact and idea, as Conrad knew, was a treacherous one: the sea finds out Jim's weakness and swallows up his character in the same way that it swallows up – as Marlow puts it – Brierly's 'reality and his sham'.

The ambivalent character of ideas is fully recognized in *Lord Jim*. On the one hand, Jim's inclination to live in a world of work-free ideas is disastrous: it prevents him from seeing what is in front of his nose:

> Each time he closed his eyes a flash of thought showed him that crowd of bodies, laid out for death, as plain as daylight. When he opened them, it was to see the dim struggle of four men fighting like mad with a stubborn boat. [LJ, 78]

While he oscillates between dream and reality, he *does* nothing. He has no Captain MacWhirr beside him, forcing him physically to grapple with reality – the presence that saves Jukes from his treacherous imagination. Unfortunately (in a sense) for Jim, the ship does not sink. The world of facts sails over the world of ideas.

Conrad however believed that there was a need for 'general thinking' which transcended the demands of immediate, concrete situations, and Jim testifies to the usefulness of such thinking in his mini-colonial war with the Sherif, where it is clear that Jim's imaginative powers are the prerequisites for victory:

> The Sherif must have thought us mad, and never troubled to come and see how we got on. Nobody believed it could be done. Why! I think the very chaps who pulled and shoved and sweated over it did not believe it could be done! Upon my word I don't think they did. [LJ, 194]

It is indeed 'upon Jim's word' that the victory is built: it is his ability imaginatively to reorder things through verbal plans that defeats the Sherif. Jim is able to go beyond the immediate reality of 'the very chaps who pulled and shoved and sweated' and to see how the Sherif can be beaten. It is small wonder that Jim's 'word' comes to be trusted, for it is above all else Jim's power of 'sustained activity' that gives him power over those who act 'almost entirely in response to the stimuli of the here and now', to use the distinction made by James Britton which I quoted in my introduction.

Lord Jim, then, reveals the inadequacy of relying solely on ideas (Jim's leap) or on brute facts (the Sherif's defeat). It also uncovers the extent to which imperialism relied upon enough ideas to subdue 'natives' and nature, while maintaining a tight hold on these ideas through a 'faith' that locked out awkward questions. That no single character is able to move between facts and ideas in a totally satisfactory way in the novel need not surprise us, for no significant social group at home or abroad in Conrad's time enjoyed this ability.

I have already mentioned Jim's relationship with language briefly, and by implication through my discussion of 'ideas'. I think that it is within this general context of 'facts and ideas' that the novel's more particular concern with language needs to be set. Throughout the novel, for example, questions about the problematic relationship between a name, and that to which it refers, are raised. It is in *Nostromo* perhaps that Conrad considers this question most exhaustively, but in fact Jim's concern with his good name is as deep as is Nostromo's. Jim's ability to use words to outwit the Sherif does not extend to his dealings with his fellow white men; he makes a mechanical equation between his name and his sense of personal identity, even when he knows that his name is the reward for keeping those amongst whom he lives in ignorance of his past history. Like Nostromo he seems more affected by being well spoken of by others, than by any inner sense of having lived up to a set of personal values. Jim, unlike Kurtz, is not eloquent:

> He was not eloquent, but there was a deep meaning in the words that followed. 'Look at these houses; there's not one where I am not trusted. Jove! I told you I would hang on. Ask any man, woman, or child.' [LJ, 181]

and again

> He was not eloquent, but there was a dignity in this constitutional reticence, there was a high seriousness in his stammerings. [LJ, 182]

Jim's attitude towards language is conditioned by his having lost his 'name'; he feels that if he can bring words back into a reliable, one-to-one relationship with facts then he will regain social acceptability and also his name. Thus his lack of eloquence testifies, as it were, to the limits of his language: he is able to see the importance of bringing words into contact with facts, but he cannot use language in any normal way as a means of discourse – even with Marlow.

> He was not speaking to me, he was only speaking before me in a dispute with an invisible personality, an antagonistic and inseparable partner of his existence – another possessor of his soul. [LJ, 68]

Although he can use language for naming, he cannot use it for real communication; when Marlow says that there was a deep meaning in his words he means that he is able to see a meaning in them, not that Jim consciously tries to communicate that meaning. Jim's inability to engage in a real dialogue (his behaviour in front of Marlow is like an externalized inner dialogue, a form of public self-address), leaves him as isolated and as much in the grip of illusions at the end of the novel as he was at the beginning: Marlow sees him leaving 'a living woman to celebrate his pitiless wedding with a shadowy ideal of conduct'.

Although by the end of the novel we learn that 'His word decided everything', Cornelius can tell Brown that Jim never lies, and this is testimony both to his honesty and to his inability to escape from the idea that, unless his words bear a constant and utterly reliable relationship with 'facts', then he will again lose his name and himself. He can confidently ask 'his' people if his words have ever brought them suffering, but he still views words as a sort of simple coinage which can be redeemed only by a direct and demonstrable relationship with concrete facts. Like the Belgians in *Heart of Darkness* he imposes words on his people, but he also imposes them on himself. He knows that he once lost his identity by losing his name, so when Dain Waris dies following Jim's 'very words', the only way he can protect his painfully constructed new identity is by dying, for this once again brings words into a direct relationship with facts: his words have died, so too must he.

> Then Jim understood. He had retreated from one world, for a small matter of an impulsive jump, and now the other, the work of his own hands, had fallen in ruins upon his head. It was not safe for his servant to go out amongst his own people! I believe that in that very moment he had decided to defy the disaster in the only way it occurred to him such a disaster could be defied; but all I know is that, without a word, he came out of his room and sat before the long table, at the head of which he was accustomed to regulate the affairs of his world, proclaiming daily the truth that surely lived in his heart. [LJ, 301]

Shortly after this he tells Tamb' Itam: 'I have no life.' He had been received, 'in a manner of speaking', by producing Stein's ring, 'into the heart of the community'. When Tamb' Itam takes the message which is to lead to Waris's death, he asks for a token: '"Because, Tuan,' he said, 'the message is important, and these are thy very words I carry."' It seems that Jim looks on his 'very words' as equivalent to his life; when he comes out of his room 'without a word' then he has no life. As Marlow expressed it, much earlier in the novel, 'from the name to the thing itself is but a step.' It is for this reason that Jim refuses to give Brown his name – a name that means something different to 'his' people who do not know of his history. But when *they* lose confidence in his word, the end has come.

Naming, as I have said, is not communication. Jim's lack of eloquence may testify to a certain honesty, but it is also related to a form of egoism. Marlow refers to his 'superb egoism' right at the end of the novel, and this is nowhere more apparent than in his attitude towards, and use of, language. He cannot speak to Marlow, but delivers a sort of private utterance to him. He interprets the words of other people as if they were aimed specifically at him. Thus the comment about the stray dog at the Inquiry – 'Look at that wretched cur' – he believes is aimed at him; and again when Brown tells him that when 'it came to saving one's life in the dark, one didn't care who else went – three, thirty, three hundred people', Jim applies the remark directly to his jump. Jim's egotistical attitude to language seems to be in direct line of descent from his earlier idealism. Idealism is a form of overestimation of the self: the idealist imposes his own mental images on the world in preference for the real nature of that world. We never see Jim engaged in real *conversation*, for his speech is all an attempt at self-expression, it does not present a view of the world for modification by another person.

This makes Jim vulnerable – not in the company of 'natives' over whom he has an advantage, but in the presence of an articulate individual such as Brown who, like other sinister characters of Conrad's such as Verloc and Peter Ivanovitch, 'knew what to say'. Marlow describes Jim as 'inarticulate' on a number of occasions, and describing his experiences in the boat after having jumped, Jim admits that 'there are no words for the sort of things I wanted to say.' Marlow, in contrast, has a very different view of the function of words. Whereas for Jim the real truths are internal, pre-verbal, and cannot without distortion be verbalized, for Marlow it is only words which give the world that order that makes it tolerable:

> For a moment I had a view of a world that seemed to wear a vast and dismal aspect of disorder, while, in truth, thanks to our unwearied efforts, it is as sunny an arrangement of small conveniences as the mind of man can conceive. But still – it was only a moment: I went back into my shell directly. One *must* – don't you know? – though I seemed to have lost all my words in the chaos of dark thoughts I had contemplated for a second or two beyond the pale. These came back too, very soon, for words also belong to the sheltering conception of light and order which is our refuge. [LJ, 230]

In one of his early meetings with Jim, Marlow notes that 'words seemed to fail him', and the statement carries a double truth. Not only does he 'dry up', but he is failed by words, for he lacks the social identity that Marlow has. Marlow can express himself in words because his words have been formed, tested and developed through collective work: as he himself says in *Heart of Darkness*, work gives one the chance to find oneself, one's own reality. Jim never finds his own reality; early on in the novel we learn:

> He loved these dreams and the success of his imaginary achievements. They were the best parts of life, its secret truth, its hidden reality. [LJ, 15]

Marlow understands that language is not just a neutral tool, but an expression of our social identity, a shared knowledge of the world that allows us to communicate with other people. Jim speaks English as if it were a foreign language, trying to find out what words mean, trying to translate them into the secret truth of his own 'hidden reality'. Even when he is writing Jim has no control over words:

> 'An awful thing has happened,' he wrote before he flung the pen down for the first time; look at the ink blot resembling the head of an arrow under these words. After a while he had tried again, scrawling heavily,

as if with a hand of lead, another line. 'I must now at once ...' The
pen had spluttered, and that time he gave it up. There's nothing more;
he had seen a broad gulf that neither eye nor voice could span. I can
understand this. He was overwhelmed by the inexplicable; he was
overwhelmed by his own personality – the gift of that destiny which
he had done his best to master. [LJ, 250]

Marlow can 'read' as much from Jim's ink blots as from his
words; Jim is overwhelmed by his personality because he has
kept his personality private, thus depriving it of verbal existence.
At this moment of crisis Jim tries to understand himself through
language, he tries to distance himself from his life-activity by
writing about himself. But he cannot. His 'scrawling', like
Kurtz's 'scrawl' at the end of the report, testifies to an inability
to objectify his own experiences. For Marlow, talk is easy:

'Talk! So be it. And it's easy enough to talk of Master Jim, after a good
spread, two hundred feet above the sea-level, with a box of decent
cigars handy, on a blessed evening of freshness and starlight.' [LJ, 26]

Marlow is a social being. Talk comes easily after the communal
activity of the meal. Jim's egoism and idealism have rendered
him mute, and the words he utters at the tribunal are to him as if
spoken by another person.

For days, for many days, he had spoken to no one, but had held silent,
incoherent, and endless converse with himself, like a prisoner alone in
his cell or like a wayfarer lost in a wilderness. At present he was answer-
ing questions that did not matter though they had a purpose, but he
doubted whether he would ever again speak out as long as he lived.
The sound of his own truthful statements confirmed his deliberate
opinion that speech was of no use to him any longer. [LJ, 24]

Words are, as Marlow puts it, a part of the order that comes from
our unwearied efforts, they belong to the sheltering conception
of light and order which is *our* refuge. Jim belongs to no collectivity. He was separated from 'the babel of voices' in the naval
officers' school by his idealism and egoism. Marlow's vision of
wordless disorder follows a comparable example of unsocial
behaviour described by Jewel, whose mother died 'speechless'
with Cornelius hammering on the door to be let in.

Tony Tanner, writing about *Falk*, relates some of these
questions to the fact of narration – a central element in Conrad's
novels as I have already argued. For if what I have said about the
collective nature of language is true, then what hope is there left
for the novelist, writing alone, for people he does not know and
to whose reactions he is not privy?

One of the processes which binds men together, as opposed to breaking
them down, is narration, the establishing of a circuit of discourse in a

particular way. Conrad's narrative technique in 'Falk' is familiar from the Marlow stories. He starts in the first person plural – 'we', 'us', 'our talk'. This strategy has three important, and illusory, effects. It conceals the solitude of writing behind the communality of conversing; it seems to transform the author into an auditor of a tale not of his making; and it makes the written text appear as a vehicle for speech.[5]

These three points are very well made, and indicate, I think, ways in which Conrad tries to avoid some of the implications that his analysis of language, speech and writing might seem to have for his own work as a novelist. The only question I would raise would be concerning Tanner's word 'illusory'. Is Conrad just effecting an illusion through operation of these techniques, or is he actually importing into written language some of the collective vitality of speech? There are several very complex issues to be argued here. For the time being I would like to suggest that, working from the contrast I have drawn between Marlow's and Jim's use of language, the building of particular language habits of an active and a collective kind can as it were 'import' an audience into written words. Marlow's speech habits are such that he uses words with a social currency to express himself; he *is* what he is through a socially available language. Jim, in contrast, has no words to express himself. Jim cannot write, because (as Vygotsky has argued in a slightly different theoretical context), before we can use words for inner cerebration and self-expression we must have developed language through dialogue with other people.

The novelist may be writing in isolation, but this need not be the same isolation as that which renders Jim inarticulate. The novelist may be possessed of the linguistic fruits of a previous, active social life. He or she may have built up a command over words in such circumstances, and be thus able to inject the life of his or her extra-literary usage into his or her novels. I believe that this is indeed true in Conrad's case, and that for all his fear and suspicion of writing – precisely because it was private and 'unreal' – his writing does feed off the 'unwearied efforts' of a more active existence. The collectivity of such an active existence – of work – may build into a person's use of language inner checks and safeguards which protect against misapplication, and thus 'unwearied efforts' in pursuit of truth can take place in the activity of the writer, as Conrad's previously quoted account of his composition of *Nostromo* would seem to suggest. Marx makes the point that when an individual is engaged in an activity which

5 Tony Tanner, "'Gnawed Bones' and 'Artless Tales' – Eating and Narrative in Conrad". In Norman Sherry (ed.), *Joseph Conrad: a Commemoration*, Macmillan, London, 1976, p. 32.

can seldom be performed in direct community with others – he cites scientific activity – he is still active socially, for the material of his activity, such as language, is given to him as a social product. Marlow, like Conrad, has such material; Jim has not.

There is another way in which a novel such as *Lord Jim* protects itself against the separation of ideas from facts which might be thought to stem from a solitary, contemplative use of language. I suggested when writing about *Heart of Darkness* that Marlow's 'adjectival insistence' drew attention both to some of the limits of language, and also to the ability of language to transcend these limits. Jim's subjective existence, like the 'heart of darkness' of Kurtz's experience in Africa, lacks a verbal identity. In both cases the narrative commentary of Marlow is a necessary stage of social transformation of these subjective experiences; Marlow can articulate his response to Jim's inarticulateness, can give it the verbal existence it lacks.

> He took his head in his hands for a moment, like a man driven to distraction by some unspeakable outrage. These were things he could not explain to the court – and not even to me; but I would have been little fitted for the reception of his confidences had I not been able at times to understand the pauses between the words. [LJ, 77]

It is not 'adjectival insistence' to call Jim's feelings of outrage 'unspeakable'; for him they are literally unspeakable because he does not have a language that can grapple effectively with his experiences. But Marlow does, and part of his unwearied effort as a narrator is devoted to imposing linguistic order on Jim's chaos of dark thoughts. It is as if Conrad is reminding the reader that he or she must be able to understand the pauses between words in the novel if he or she is to be deemed suited for the reception of confidences. Marlow tells his listeners that they may be able better to tell whether his commonplace fears were unjust, 'since the proverb has it that the onlookers see most of the game' [LJ, 164]. The remark, casually tossed off, is profoundly important. Not only does Marlow understand Jim better than he understands himself, but his listeners understand Marlow better than he understands the events he relates – and perhaps the reader understands more of Conrad's 'game' than he does himself. The suggestion is not made lightly, nor in criticism of Conrad. It rests on a theory of meaning that seems, at least in part, to have been shared by Conrad himself: meaning is not images or sensations in individual minds, but what is publicly expressible in or abstractable from words. Edward Said, talking in fact about *Heart of Darkness* although his words apply equally well to *Lord Jim*, suggests that

What Marlow does in the tale is precisely – or as precisely as he can – to name something which has no name; he does this in order for it to be seen.[6]

Marlow does not, in *Lord Jim*, believe that he has named anything either completely or finally, however.

> Besides, the last word is not said – probably never shall be said. Are not our lives too short for that full utterance which through all our stammerings is of course our only and abiding intention? I have given up expecting those last words, whose ring, if they could only be pronounced, would shake both heaven and earth. There is never time to say our last word – the last word of our love, of our desire, faith, remorse, submission, revolt. . . . My last words about Jim shall be few. I affirm he had achieved greatness; but the thing would be dwarfed in the telling, or rather in the hearing. Frankly, it is not my words that I mistrust but your minds. I could be eloquent were I not afraid you fellows had starved your imaginations to feed your bodies. I do not mean to be offensive; it is respectable to have no illusions – and safe – and profitable – and dull. Yet you, too, in your time must have known the intensity of life, that light of glamour created in the shock of trifles, as amazing as the glow of sparks struck from a cold stone – and as short-lived, alas. [LJ, 165]

If Marlow does not say the last word, the reader must understand the pauses between his words, must bring his or her own understanding to the incompletenesses and absences of Marlow's narration. Marlow *affirms* rather than *tells of* Jim's greatness, and the reader must not expect to reconstitute Jim's greatness from Marlow's words alone. The passage suggests that, although Marlow is able to verbalize things Jim cannot express in words because he lacks a language forged through collective activity, the collective activity of Marlow's listeners is also limited, and thus they are not fitted to receive an account of Jim's greatness. Jim's greatness for Marlow seems to be comparable to Kurtz's 'affirmation' and 'moral victory'. In both cases the self is sacrificed in order to contribute to a collective understanding.

At the end of his narrative Marlow looks at his listeners, 'with the eyes of a man returning from the excessive remoteness of a dream'. Just as Jim's dream is understood rather than experienced by Marlow, so too Marlow's dream must be understood by us. 'Feeling' and 'understanding' must never be confused:

> Yes! few of us understand, but we all feel it though, and I say *all* without exception, because those who do not feel do not count. Each blade of grass has its spot on earth whence it draws its life, its strength; and so is man rooted to the land from which he draws his faith together with his life. I don't know how much Jim understood; but I know he

6 Edward W. Said, 'Conrad and Nietzsche'. In Sherry, *op. cit.*, p. 70.

felt, he felt confusedly but powerfully, the demand of some such truth or some such illusion – I don't care how you call it, there is so little difference, and the difference means so little. [LJ, 163]

It means so little to one's feelings – but so much to one's understanding!

The passage above testifies to the collective rather than individual nature of understanding, but in its relating of 'faith' to national identity it also reminds us of Marlow's previously quoted comment on the faith which is invulnerable to the strength of facts, the contagion of example and the solicitation of ideas. Jim's consciousness is the 'faith' of imperialist Britain, a consciousness that understands enough to change the material world and dominate 'natives', but which is still 'rooted to the land' and *unable to understand itself* because it cannot displace itself from itself. Jim can use words to defeat the Sherif, but he cannot speak articulately to other white men.

Marlow's admonitions to his listeners, I would argue, have the effect of reminding the reader of the novel that in reading the novel he or she must not just soak up feelings from it, but must attempt to understand it. There are other points in the novel where the reader is, indirectly, reminded of the responsibilities of the reader. Writing to Richard Curle the year before his own death, Conrad drew a parallel between his writing and Marconi's radio transmissions, noting that

Marconi's electric waves could [not] be made evident without the sending-out and receiving instruments. In other words, without mankind my art, an infinitesimal thing, could not exist. [CTAF, 191]

This relating of the art of the novel to 'sending-out and receiving instruments', rather than to reified or hypostatized 'works' or words is evidenced within *Lord Jim*. Just as Marlow's comments on his own narrative draw the reader's attention to Conrad's art as novelist, so too Marlow's statements about the act of writing are similarly evocative of certain normally suppressed thoughts on the part of the reader.

I found out how difficult it may be sometimes to make a sound. There is a weird power in a spoken word. And why the devil not? I was asking myself persistently while I drove on with my writing. All at once, on the blank page, under the very point of the pen, the two figures of Chester and his antique partner, very distinct and complete, would dodge into view with stride and gestures, as if reproduced in the field of some optical toy. I would watch them for a while. No! They were too phantasmal and extravagant to enter into any one's fate. And a word carries far – very far – deals destruction through time as the bullets go flying through space. [LJ, 128]

If the immediate meaning of these words for the reader lies in Marlow's deliberations about whether Jim can safely be left to tender mercies of Chester and his partner, an insistent secondary one suggests itself. The passage has the appearance of being a sort of meta-commentary by Conrad on the process of writing a novel. Should the two characters be given fictional existence? Should Conrad 'write them in to' the novel? If this suggestion seems far-fetched it is worth making the point that passages involving such an ambiguity of semantic level occur more and more frequently in Conrad's work, culminating in the most self-conscious of Conrad's novels, *Under Western Eyes*. I find it hard to rid myself of the feeling that the passage, in addition to describing Marlow's rather avuncular defence of Jim's interests, also gives us Conrad's supra-fictional commentary on the creative process itself. Marlow is sitting writing while Jim is in an adjoining room, and the whole scene of which this passage forms a part could describe Conrad's decision not to terminate his tale at this point (*Lord Jim* was originally intended to be a short story), but to continue it further.

> To bury him would have been such an easy kindness! It would have been so much in accordance with the wisdom of life, which consists in putting out of sight all the reminders of our folly, of our weakness, of our mortality; all that makes against our efficiency – the memory of our failures, the hints of our undying fears, the bodies of our dead friends. Perhaps he did take it too much to heart. And if so then – Chester's offer. . . . At this point I took up a fresh sheet and began to write resolutely. [LJ, 127]

If this last-quoted passage does not seem to communicate on two levels – one of which comments upon the other – then I would only ask that the reader of this book maintain an open mind on the subject. My own conviction that it does is in part the result of the cumulative effect of a number of such passages. If I am right, it certainly suggests that there is an autobiographical element in *Lord Jim* rather different from that which the simple identification of 'Patna' with 'Poland' – which has been suggested – might indicate. Why 'the bodies of our dead friends'? The phrase makes no sense other than of a vague reference to an undeclared memory of Marlow's – and what is that shown to have to do with the matter of 'disposing' of Jim?

'A word is like a bullet.' Its meaning is not necessarily the intention of the person who utters, or writes, it. In *Heart of Darkness* bursting shells were described as an ominous voice; here a word is likened to a bullet. The bullet 'means' what it does to its recipient, as well as what the person who pulls the trigger intends. The simile not only draws our attention to the power of words, but to their arbitrary quality, their ability to exist independently from the person who utters them – as with the chance remark about the 'wretched cur'. Was it because Conrad, like Marlow, had doubts about 'receiving instruments', about the imaginations of his readers, that he felt the need to remind them of this fact? Is it Marlow – or Conrad – who concludes that Jim is an oddly insubstantial figure at times?

> Now he is no more, there are days when the reality of his existence comes to me with an immense, with an overwhelming force; and yet upon my honour there are moments, too, when he passes from my eyes like a disembodied spirit astray amongst the passions of this earth, ready to surrender himself faithfully to the claim of his own world of shades. [LJ, 307]

Lord Jim serves to illustrate the fact that the human relationships and experiences of people are not just 'there' to be described in a waiting language. They emerge from and exist within linguistic potentialities, and they react back upon these potentialities. Novels like *Heart of Darkness* and *Lord Jim* remind us, too, that the degree to which a reader actively participates in the world, and exploits potentialities presented to him or her by the socio-linguistic community to which he or she belongs, can be as important as the extent to which the novelist has similarly exploited the potentialities made available to him or her.

3

Nostromo: materialism and idealism

> Material changes swept along in the train of material interests. And other changes more subtle, outwardly unmarked, affected the minds and hearts of the workers. [N, 504]

Given the above quotation out of context, and asked to comment on its likely textual origin, it's not hard to imagine someone being grossly wrong. A little known writing by Marx? A piece of Communist propaganda? In fact it is from *Nostromo*, the novel in which the apparently 'Communist' character, the 'bloodthirsty hater of capitalists', is portrayed as a humourless, sinister, jargonizing freak. Yet the quotation is not used by Conrad to mock the ideas it contains; it indeed summarizes reasonably accurately a theme that runs through the novel both in the larger movements of plot and also in narrative comments which appear to carry substantial authorial authority. How is this apparent contradiction to be explained?

Conrad, I would argue, is fundamentally a materialist, but politically he is consistently a conservative. The combination may seem odd to us today, but I suspect it was less odd in Conrad's time. An additional complicating factor is undoubtedly Conrad's Polish background, which, as Zdzistaw Najder suggests,

> made Conrad a man disinherited, lonely, and (for a Western writer of that time) exceptionally conscious of the sinister brutalities hidden behind the richly ornate facade of *bourgeois* political optimism. And these characteristics are precisely what makes Conrad our contemporary. [CPB, 31]

The historic compromise between aristocracy and bourgeoisie that had taken place in Britain had not taken place in Poland; Conrad's conservatism does not lead him in the direction that it would have led, most probably, a native-born Englishman. But neither do his materialism and atheism lead him in the direction, politically, that they would have led such a person. The Englishman born and bred who could have written the above words from *Nostromo*, and who could have written to a friend that from the age of fourteen he had always disliked the Christian religion, and was galled by the fact that 'not a single Bishop of them' believes in it – 'The business in the stable isn't convincing' [LFC, 188] – such a one would surely have resembled Conrad's friend Cunninghame Graham, an aristocratic socialist. Conrad is in many ways such an interesting writer because his opinions and philosophy are not mechanically correlated with any overtly political position. I do not mean to suggest by this that there were not political ramifications to his opinions or philosophy, but that politics in Britain was so foreign to him that he tended to take a wider view than might have been inspired by a party-political allegiance or sympathy.

Let me say a few words about what I mean by Conrad's materialism. By this I do not mean to evoke the everyday, pejorative usage of this word to suggest a self-interested seeking after material gain. I mean a philosophical view that matter is primary, that it precedes consciousness, which is a special property of matter and does not exist independently of matter.

The most impressive, even moving, declaration of such principles that I know of comes not from a textbook of Marxist philosophy, but from Conrad's 'Author's Note' to *The Shadow-Line*, where he answers the suggestion that in this work he had taken his imagination beyond the confines of the world of living, suffering humanity, and included a supernatural element therein.

> I could never have attempted such a thing, because all my moral and intellectual being is penetrated by an invincible conviction that whatever falls under the dominion of our senses must be in nature and, however exceptional, cannot differ in its essence from all the other effects of the visible and tangible world of which we are a self-conscious part. The world of the living contains enough marvels and mysteries as it is; marvels and mysteries acting upon our emotions and intelligence in ways so inexplicable that it would almost justify the conception of life as an enchanted state. [TSL, v]

As I have said before, whatever solipsistic pressures Conrad may have been subject to, he understood these as forces which cut him off from a world which he knew existed, and of which he believed himself to be a self-conscious part – very different from actually entertaining doubts about the existence of the 'visible and tangible world' of other people.

Not only does Conrad have a firm conviction that human beings are a self-conscious part of nature, he also – as my opening quotation demonstrates – has a view of the forces which cause that self-conscious part to change. The hierarchy of influence and determination is clearly set out in this quotation: material interests sweep along material changes in their train, and other changes affect the minds and hearts of the workers. If against this passage we set a famous passage by Marx and Engels from *The German Ideology* the parallel is striking:

> The ideas of the ruling class are in every epoch the ruling ideas, i.e. the class which is the ruling *material* force of society, is at the same time its ruling *intellectual* force. . . . The ruling ideas are nothing more than the ideal expression of the dominant material relationships, the dominant material relationships grasped as ideas.[1]

Although there is some evidence that Conrad had direct or indirect acquaintance with Marx's writings (Avrom Fleishman has pointed out the resemblance that Michaelis's speech at the opening of chapter three of *The Secret Agent* bears to a famous passage in Marx's *The Eighteenth Brumaire of Louis Bonaparte*),[2] I do not feel that an attempt to trace 'influences' is a particularly fruitful project here. What is important is a study of the artistic and aesthetic development of Conrad's ideas.

What seems to me to be the core achievement of *Nostromo* is the searching, delicate investigation into the relationship between material interests, material changes, and the hearts and minds of characters that it presents us with. Like *Lord Jim*, *Nostromo* is concerned with relationships between facts and ideas, with the complex and dialectical interplay between material and intellectual forces. The novel certainly suggests that ideas have force only to the extent that they have material interests behind them, to the extent that they are the embodiment of material forces. (Marx's 'ruling ideas' can be taken two ways – either the ideas which dominate intellectual life, or the ideas through which the ruling class rules.) We are told that Gould's 'word' is law not because it is intellectually convincing, but because behind it it has the power of the silver. Indeed, we are even told that Gould's silences had as many shades of meaning as uttered words and that an affirmative nod of his head was taken as a verbal contract

> which men had learned to trust implicitly, since behind it all there was the great San Tomé mine, the head and front of the material interests, so strong that it depended on no man's goodwill in the whole length and breadth of the Occidental Province – that is, on no goodwill which it could not buy ten times over. [N, 203]

1 Karl Marx and Frederick Engels, *The German Ideology*, part 1. Edited and with an introduction by C. J. Arthur, Lawrence and Wishart, London, 1970, p. 64.
2 Avrom Fleishman, *op. cit.*, p. 210. Writing to Cunninghame Graham on 19 January 1900, Conrad comments: 'Of course there is a material basis for every state of mind, and so for mine' [LCG, 131]. It is hard to imagine his writing to many of his other correspondents in these terms.

In contrast, the intellectually honest, sincerely wrought pages of *Fifty Years of Misrule* – "impartial and eloquent' as Conrad ironically and damningly puts it in his Author's Note to the novel – are utterly powerless to influence the real course of events in the novel because behind them no comparable material interests are to be found. *Fifty Years of Misrule* is as important a symbol of the powerlessness of disembodied words as is Kurtz's report in *Heart of Darkness*, although in a rather different way. In the midst of social upheaval, with political brutality threatening, Charles Gould meets Don Juste – the character in *Nostromo* who most effectively portrays the hollowness of liberal principles and ideals when they are separated from material interests. Gould advises against an accommodation with the new 'authorities', but is dismayed by the effect of his words on these men:

> [He] stopped before the sad bewilderment of the faces, the wondering, anxious glances of the eyes. The feeling of pity for those men, putting all their trust into words of some sort, while murder and rapine stalked over the land, had betrayed him into what seemed empty loquacity. [N, 367]

Putting your trust in words is not much use if they have no material interests behind them.

Andrzez Busza is one critic who has argued explicitly against seeing Conrad as a materialist:

> An important theme of Conrad's work is the notion that reality is illusory and that life is only a dream. . . . It is clearly incompatible with any genuine materialistic philosophy.[3]

To this I would make two replies – firstly that I find no evidence in Conrad's writings that he considered that 'reality is illusory' (either an odd claim or an odd way of expressing it) and, secondly, that the notion that life is only a dream certainly does occur frequently in Conrad's writings, but should not be taken as evidence that he considered reality to be illusory. The notion is a complicated one, but at base I think that in talking about life as a dream Conrad is referring to the experiential, 'non-displaced' aspects of human life. Such a notion is complemented, I believe, by the notion that man can examine his dreams, that through such detached scrutiny he can come to know more about that reality of which he is a self-conscious part.

Conrad may be a materialist, in the sense that I have suggested, but he is not in any way a crude or mechanical materialist. If in

---

3 Andrzez Busza, 'Conrad's Polish Literary Background and some Illustrations of the Influence of Polish Literature on his Work'. *Antemcerale*, Rome and London, 1966, p. 134.

Nostromo he makes it clear that it is material interests rather than words which determine the movement of history, this does not mean that words are to be seen as unimportant. In fact one of the most notable aspects of *Nostromo* is Conrad's detailed attention to the problem of ideology, that is to the way in which material interests 'use' ideas to obtain power. Consider a striking example: Decoud realizes that unless a constant flow of silver is kept up from Costaguana to the United States then Holroyd's backing for the separationist movement – which Decoud sees as his last chance – will not be forthcoming. But although he perceives the necessity for arguments and persuasion to be backed by ingots, he also understands well that this fundamental satisfaction of Holroyd's material interests will be transposed by Holroyd into a different, intellectual form, given ideological existence in order better to be able to conceal its own nature. Put simply, Holroyd will be convinced by material facts which pander to his material interests, but will deceive himself about this.

> But then there was that other sentimentalist, who attached a strangely idealistic meaning to concrete facts. This stream of silver must be kept flowing north to return in the form of financial backing from the great house of Holroyd. [N, 219]

Conrad's significant insight in *Nostromo* is to have seen that although, fundamentally, it is material interests not ideas that effect historical change, material interests effect this change through ideas. A comparable paradox is the fact that although it is men like Holroyd and Gould who are the tools of material interests, they are themselves the most idealistic of men, like Keats's two brothers in 'Isabella', at least half-ignorant of their true motives or of what they are doing. Indeed, *Nostromo* suggests that in certain cases the greater the self-deception practised by an individual the more use he or she will be to material interests.

This, I think, explains why *Nostromo* at times seems to present a rather deterministic world-view. Characters such as Holroyd and Gould are mistaken about their motives, about what they are doing. They are, in a fundamental sense, tools of forces they do not fully comprehend. In contrast to this, Dr Monygham has a clearer view of relationships between material forces and historical change, but except at odd moments he is not able to intervene in the changes that are taking place. It is arguable, however, that this was a pretty accurate reflection of politics both in Europe and in South America in Conrad's time, when the clearest-sighted were not always the nearest to power.

Charles Gould's idealism is in direct line of descent from that of his father. Like Jim, Mr Gould senior escaped into 'light literature', and Conrad associates this self-deception with the start of his enslavement by material interests.

> Mr Gould had swallowed the pill, and it was as though it had been compounded of some subtle poison that acted directly on his brain. He became at once mine-ridden, and as he was well read in light literature it took to his mind the form of the Old Man of the Sea fastened upon his shoulders. [N, 55]

Mr Gould's son also becomes mine-ridden, but instead of the mine taking the form of the Old Man of the Sea, it becomes as a mistress to him, usurping the place of his wife in his thoughts and affections. Talking to his wife, Decoud tells her that her husband is an idealist.

> 'Charley an idealist!' she said, as if to herself, wonderingly. 'What on earth do you mean?'
> 'Yes,' conceded Decoud, 'it's a wonderful thing to say with the sight of the San Tomé mine, the greatest fact in the whole of South America, perhaps, before our very eyes. But look even at that, he has idealized this fact to a point –' He paused. 'Mrs Gould, are you aware to what point he has idealized the existence, the worth, the meaning of the San Tomé mine? Are you aware of it?'
> He must have known what he was talking about.
> The effect he expected was produced. Mrs Gould, ready to take fire, gave it up suddenly with a low little sound that resembled a moan.
> 'What do you know?' she asked in a feeble voice.
> 'Nothing,' answered Decoud, firmly. 'But, then, don't you see, he's an Englishman?'
> 'Well, what of that?' asked Mrs Gould.
> 'Simply that he cannot act or exist without idealizing every simple feeling, desire, or achievement. *He could not believe his own motives if he did not make them first a part of some fairy tale.* The earth is not quite good enough for him, I fear. [N, 214; my italics]

I quote this passage at length because of its unequivocal association of Gould's idealism with his nationality: it is because the English are at the time of Conrad's writing *the* imperialist nation that the English cannot act without idealizing feelings, desires and achievements. What this passage describes is a process of ideological displacement – a half-ignorant control of material forces through the construction of convincing fairy tales. That these fairy tales destroy Gould's relationship with his wife and his inner life is further evidence of Conrad's deep insight into the ramifications of such ideological displacement. Decoud understands that such fairy tales are not just a by-product of material interests, but are the very means whereby these interests effect their goals. Writing to his sister he explains that

> [the Goulds'] sentiment was necessary to the very life of my plan; the sentimentalism of the people that will never do anything for the sake of their passionate desire, unless it comes to them clothed in the fair robes of an idea. [N, 239]

The suggestion is not a new one in Conrad's work: the whole force of *Heart of Darkness* works to a similar conclusion, that the passionate desires of the imperialists had to be clothed in the fair robes of ideas about civilizing missions.

It should be said, however, that Conrad did differentiate between British imperialism – which he considered had an 'idea' behind it – and the imperialist ventures of such as the Belgians. Writing to Mrs Aniela Zagorska (in Polish), Conrad says of the Boers, at the time of the Boer War:

> That they are struggling in good faith for their independence cannot be doubted; but it is also a fact that they have no idea of liberty, which can only be found under the English flag all over the world. [CPB, 232]

He denies that the government is sending English soldiers (presumably against their will), and argues in support of this that Canada and Australia are taking part in this war, 'which could not affect their material interests'. He thus seems to have believed that the English did have a relatively disinterested approach to matters of international politics which was lacked by other nations. Decoud's view of the 'sentimentalism' of the English can therefore be taken in two ways – either as evidence of a change of heart on Conrad's part, or as a realization that the good intentions of the English were no defence against their appropriation by material interests. Whether Decoud's comments are meant to be taken as exemplary of the cynicism of other nations, or as a true insight into the self-deceptive powers of the English, is hard to determine. In the context of *Nostromo*, however, there is no doubt that Decoud is right about Charles Gould.

There is a grim appropriateness in the two bookcases in the Casa Gould, one full of books and one full of weaponry; Gould is aware of the need to trust in God and keep his powder dry – even to convince himself that he is trusting in God when he is actually keeping his powder dry. Gould does not live absolutely in a fairy tale. He has a certain knowledge of the realities of the situation in which he finds himself, but because he does idealize his own role in it he finds it, when he perceives it clearly, tragic:

> Unlike Decoud, Charles Gould could not play lightly a part in a tragic farce. It was tragic enough for him in all conscience, but he could see no farcical element. He suffered too much under a conviction of irremediable folly. *He was too severely practical and too idealistic to*

look upon its terrible humours with amusement, as Martin Decoud, the imaginative materialist, was able to do in the dry light of his scepticism. [N, 364; my italics]

The blend of practicality and idealism in Charles Gould is not just an interesting personal trait, a mixture of qualities that makes him an interesting and unique 'character'. It is necessary for the role he has to play, making him able to understand enough to manipulate nature and 'natives', without being bothered by what he is doing.

As Decoud says, 'It's a part of solid English sense not to think too much; to see only what may be of practical use at the moment.' Or as Marlow put it in *Lord Jim*, 'Hang ideas!'

In *Nostromo*, as in many of Conrad's other novels, much is made of the idealism of women. As with Marlow's aunt and the Intended in *Heart of Darkness*, the ideological function that this performs is made apparent, and indicates the sort of usefulness that the different idealism of the men has. It is nice to have womenfolk who have illusions about what one is doing when one doesn't want fully to admit to oneself the truth about it. One knows, as Marlow and Gould know, that the women are wrong: they live in a beautiful world of their own. But it's nice to have that world there – not to live in, for as Marlow says in *Heart of Darkness*, 'if they were to set it up it would go to pieces before the first sunset', but to convince one that one has higher ideals than sometimes seems to be the case.

> Even the most legitimate touch of materialism was wanting in Mrs Gould's character. The dead man of whom she thought with tenderness (because he was Charley's father) and with some impatience (because he had been weak), must be put completely in the wrong. Nothing else would do to keep their prosperity without a stain on its only real, on its immaterial side! [N, 75]

Mrs Gould's idealism is to her husband's practicality as his own idealism is to his political clear-sightedness; this structured, many levelled idealism has the function of keeping their prosperity unstained, and – by keeping it unstained – keeping it.

If the silver can work its effect on hearts and minds – of Holroyd and Gould as well as of 'the workers' – only through ideas, these ideas can themselves have currency only through their constitution in words. Words without the backing of material interests may be vain, but material interests need words to gain sway over the hearts and minds of men. Holroyd sees the export of words to be as necessary for his purposes as the export of capital or mining equipment:

> We shall be giving the word for everything: industry, trade, law,

journalism, art, politics, and religion, from Cape Horn clear over to Smith's Sound, and beyond, too, if anything worth taking hold of turns up at the North Pole. [N, 77]

'Giving the word,' as Holroyd sees it, is a necessary preliminary to 'taking hold of' anything that turns up. The phrase has an intriguing ambiguity about it, suggesting not just the indication of 'approval to proceed', but also an imposition of alien linguistic forms on subject peoples not dissimilar to that which Conrad outlined in *Heart of Darkness*. The phrase also makes it clear that the linguistic process is a one-way, non-reciprocal one. 'Giving the word' is not engaging in dialogue but telling people, and the mélange of activities which follows this phrase is a pointer to Holroyd's philistinism in its mixing of journalism and law with art and industry.

'Giving the word' does, however, have other reverberations. Industrialization and the societies to which it gives rise rely more heavily on precise verbal expression than on non-verbal forms of communication. The reasons for this are complex, but they include the increasing importance of communication through signs and over temporal and geographical distances, the importance of precision in instructions – so that interchangable words and terms parallel the development of interchangable machine parts – and the more general need for abstractions and generalizations which industrialization brings with it. This process may be relatively unremarked within one society, but colonialism and imperialism have the effect of bringing it into sharp relief. I have been told by a Nigerian who has lived in Britain for over ten years that she has come to rely on words, rather than non-verbal expression, far more in Britain, and that when she returns to Nigeria people comment upon how 'verbal' she has become. 'Giving the word' can have a wider sense than just imposing an alien set of meanings upon a people; it can involve planting the seeds of a far more 'verbal' culture.

Holroyd's faith in words is as philistine as his last speech would suggest, however. Words are useful enough to encourage the exportation of silver, but not to consider the larger questions that this exportation raises. We are told that by his previous speech (the section I quoted was only a part of the whole speech),

he meant to express his faith in destiny in words suitable to his intelligence, which was unskilled in the presentation of general ideas. His intelligence was nourished on facts; and Charles Gould, whose imagination had been permanently affected by the one great fact of a silver mine, had no objection to this theory of the world's future. [N, 77]

As the quotation from Perry Anderson which I considered at

the end of my discussion of *Heart of Darkness* made clear, exploitation of subject peoples needed a certain level of practical skill, but 'general ideas' raised too many awkward questions.

Decoud, talking to Antonia, suggests that the economic exploitation of their country has been based on a gap of knowledge on the part of those initiating the exploitation:

> 'Just imagine our forefathers in morions and corselets drawn up outside this gate, and a band of adventurers just landed from their ships in the harbour there. Thieves, of course. Speculators, too. Their expeditions, each one, were the speculations of grave and reverend persons in England. That is history, as that absurd sailor Mitchell is always saying.' [N, 174]

The gap of knowledge between the speculations of grave and reverend persons in England, and the actions of thieves in South America, is a gap of knowledge that Captain Mitchell is quite right to describe as history. Like the sailors in the French man-of-war in *Heart of Darkness*, the speculators are the initiators of actions the results of which they do not witness. Holroyd too sets wheels in motion, and the wheels duly provide him with a flow of silver and moral reassurance: what goes on in the heart of the machine is concealed from his gaze and his understanding. 'Speculation' can of course have two meanings – a financial risk taken in expectation of profit, and an imaginative sortie into the realms of the possible. It is the ability of human beings to speculate, to imagine states of affairs other than those that they are actually experiencing, that allows of the financial sort of speculation. And it is this sort of speculation which can set the wheels of imperialism in motion.

The difference between Charles Gould and those reverend persons in England is that he is on the spot in South America, and they are not. There is no problem for them: like Holroyd they pump in money and platitudes and receive back more wealth and gratification. There is no problem for the thieves, who also knew what they were doing. But Gould is in the awkward position that Kurtz was in, having the illusions of the grave and reverend persons, but having them dispelled by the immediate reality he cannot but witness. It is all very well for Holroyd to 'give the word'; Gould has to live with the word, and he finds that it assumes a different appearance on South American soil:

> The words one knows so well have a nightmarish meaning in this country. Liberty, democracy, patriotism, government – all of them have a flavour of folly and murder. [N, 408]

Gould does not realize that his own gift of words to his wife involves the same transposition. As we learn at the start of the novel, he 'did not open his heart to [his wife] in any set speeches', but 'simply went on acting and thinking in her sight'. Conrad ironically adds that this 'is the true method of sincerity' – but the reader knows better. Sincerity is engaging in open dialogue. Talking and acting 'in front of' someone is not sincerity but egoism, the egoism of Jim, for example, or Kurtz, both of whom behave in precisely this way. Gould and his wife only really communicate by defining their common interests against the different interests of others:

> Their confidential intercourse fell, not in moments of privacy, but precisely in public, when the quick meeting of their glances would comment upon some fresh turn of events. [N, 165]

Their intimacy is not a fully human discovery of each other through common attempts to subdue what Conrad calls nature, but is a narrowly political sharing of private cultural interest. It is as if their adoption for use as convenient tools by material interests has deprived them of an identity apart from this function. Gould pins his hopes to the strengthening of material interests without realizing that this very strengthening diminishes him as a human being – although his wife comes to understand that this is the case.

Towards the end of the novel Mrs Gould asks Dr Monygham whether there will ever be any peace or rest.

> 'No!' interrupted the doctor. 'There is no peace and no rest in the development of material interests. They have their law, and their justice. But it is founded on expediency, and is inhuman; it is without rectitude, without the continuity and the force that can be found only in a moral principle.' [N, 511]

The statement is a powerful indictment of that indirect mediation of human contact through material interests that Gould champions at the start of the novel. Monygham puts his finger on it: it is *inhuman*. When human interests are personified in material interests they are, effectively, lost. Gould's moral decline is traceable from the early point where he starts to treat the mine as if it were a person – and his wife as if she were not.

> '[Holroyd] may have to give in, or he may have to die tomorrow, but the great silver and iron interests shall survive, and some day shall get hold of Costaguana along with the rest of the world.'
> They had stopped near the cage. The parrot, catching the sound of a word belonging to his vocabulary, was moved to interfere. Parrots are very human.
> 'Viva Costaguana!' he shrieked, with intense self-assertion. [N, 82]

In as much as Gould is right that the great silver and iron interests are more powerful than any man, then without the backing of these material interests his own words have no more force than a parrot's. His statement is almost a glorification of the weakness of individual human beings in the face of objects of wealth. To the extent that Gould becomes an appendage of the material interests so do his words become no more human than the words of the parrot. Conrad uses the parrot's talk throughout his novels and letters as a symbol of the unthinking use of words. The example points to one of the odd things about words, that they can be used unthinkingly and yet can still have an effect on an auditor. Vygotsky makes an analogous point rather neatly in talking about the different significance that a word can have for a child and an adult. The child interprets the word in terms of a narrow *reference* to a thing, like a proper name, while for the adult the word has a *meaning* – it can be incorporated into a wider structure of significance. Vygotsky points out that when a child talks to an adult the words both use will coincide in their reference but not in their meaning. The words of grave and reverend persons in England, and adventurers in South America can also coincide in their reference but not their meaning, as Charles Gould is brought to discover.

It is an important part of the meaning of *Nostromo* that Nostromo's own relationship to language turns from one of a child, where words are seen to have a simple reference to things, to one in which he begins to be aware of the treacherous use that can be made of words. Decoud notices how important it is for Nostromo that he is well spoken of, and adds that Nostromo appears not to make any distinction between thinking and speaking. Jim, we remember, suffered from a similar limitation of understanding. Decoud is at this point making reference to Nostromo's attitude to what other people say, but at times the reader of the novel is led to feel that Nostromo is at first incapable of conceiving of duplicity in words. Decoud is unsure whether Nostromo's attitude is the result of naivety or practicality, and it's probably true that taking everything at face value (what a revealing phrase that is!) has its advantages. Señora Teresa at one point charges Nostromo with being away fighting for what did not concern him:

> 'Why talk like this?' mumbled the Capataz between his teeth.
> 'Will you never believe in my good sense? It concerns me to keep on being what I am: every day alike.'
>
> 'You never change, indeed,' she said, bitterly. 'Always thinking of yourself and taking your pay out in fine words from those who care nothing for you.' [N, 253]

The comparison of words to pay is instructive: words are used as things with exchange value, rather than mediators between human beings which have a shared human significance. Nostromo, of course, at this point in the novel believes that this is what the words he is 'paid' in have, that they testify to a particular human identity that he has attained to. But Señora Teresa is right; the words he is given do not have the meaning for those who utter them that they have for Nostromo. He is treated like a child; the words have a common reference for Nostromo and his paymasters, but their meaning is not shared.

That Nostromo is known by three different names as the novel proceeds is not accidental. Signora Teresa laughs at the name 'Nostromo' early on in the novel, remarking cuttingly that 'he would take a name that is properly no word from them', and in Nostromo's refusal to be called by this name at the house of the Violas (of which the reader learns later on) there is evidence of Nostromo's recognition of the function that this name plays. After he has begun to realize how he has been used, following his swim back to Sulaco, he displays 'a reluctance to pronounce the name by which he was known'. Like Jim he associates personal identity so closely with his name – like a child seeing a name as an attribute of a thing or person rather than a sign – that in order to construct himself another public existence he has to adopt a new name, 'Capataz de Cargadores'. Whereas Decoud is described as the man with no faith in anything except the truth of his own sensations, Nostromo puts all his faith not in material interests but in words.

Once Nostromo begins to realize the inadequacy of his previous attitude to words, then other significant changes in him take place:

> What he had heard Georgio Viola say once was very true. Kings, ministers, aristocrats, the rich in general, kept the people in poverty and subjection; they kept them as they kept dogs, to fight and hunt for their service. [N, 415]

Writing to Cunninghame Graham, Conrad suggested that Nostromo was not to be considered a fully realized, individual character:

> But truly N[ostromo] is nothing at all – a fiction – embodied vanity of the sailor kind – a romantic mouthpiece of 'the people' which (I mean 'the people') frequently experience the very feelings to which he gives utterance. I do not defend him as a creation. [LCG, 157]

If Nostromo is taken to be representative of the people, then his failure to be able to manipulate words – or to see how words are manipulated – may be taken as Conrad's understanding of the linguistic disabilities of the people in general. Basil Bernstein's distinction between working-class and middle-class speech – for all its shortcomings and inadequacies – draws attention to a relevant point:

> Historically, and now, only a tiny percentage of the population has been socialized into knowledge at the level of the meta-languages of control and innovation, whereas the mass of the population has been socialized into knowledge at the level of context-tied operations.[4]

Those who 'give the word' have control of such meta-languages, although their knowledge and control do not extend to the larger forces that shape their own lives, as we see with Charles Gould. But they do have control over the mine, and they do have control over Nostromo, who is certainly an example at the beginning of the novel of a person who is socialized into knowledge at the level of context-tied operations.

Bernstein distinguishes between what he calls 'restricted' and 'elaborated' codes, and it is the latter which he sees giving the power of control and innovation through separation from context-bound utterance. The distinction has important points of contact with Marx's distinction between the animal which is a part of its life activity, and man who can make his life activity the subject of his scrutiny. By the end of the novel Nostromo has burst through into a perception of his previous enslavement – has succeeded in distancing himself from his life activity – but has discovered that this involves losses as well as gains. Bernstein notes:

> Elaborated codes give access to alternative realities, yet they carry the potential of alienation, of feeling from thought, of self from other, of private belief *from role obligation*.[5]

Whereas at the start of the novel Nostromo *was* the role he played, by the end of the novel his public self is separate from his private self.

> A transgression, a crime, entering a man's existence, eats it up like a malignant growth, consumes it like a fever. Nostromo had lost his peace; the genuineness of all his qualities was destroyed. He felt it himself, and often cursed the silver of San Tomé. His courage, his magnificence, his leisure, his work, everything was as before, only everything was a sham. [N, 523]

In Nostromo's eventual fate we see mirrored the choice 'the people' had in Conrad's day – context-bound in their under-

4 Basil Bernstein, 'Social Class, Language and Socialization'. Reprinted in *Class, Codes and Control* I, Paladin edn, Frogmore, St Albans, reprinted 1973, p. 199.
5 Bernstein, *op. cit.*, p. 212.

standing but relatively undivided if exploited, or possessed of 'meta-languages of control and innovation' but alienated and divided from themselves. This should not be taken to mean, as some of Bernstein's simpler detractors have suggested, that access to abstractions and the ability to distance oneself from one's life activity are bad things. Nostromo is corrupted because his achievement of self-knowledge is bound up with an accession of wealth that separates his interests from those of his fellows, and it is still true today that the same achievement of self-consciousness and imaginative control over 'alternative realities' is often sought for private rather than disinterested motives. The answer is not to reject such control, but to enable it to be exercised in the interests of all.

Nostromo's relationship with Giselle is destroyed by the silver. He cannot be open and frank with her about it, cannot trust her, and she has a 'sense of unreality and deception' instead of bliss and security in her intercourse with her promised husband. Mrs Gould has already had a similar experience:

> The fate of the San Tomé mine was lying heavy upon [Mrs. Gould's] heart. It was a long time now since she had begun to fear it. It had been an idea. She had watched it with misgivings turning into a fetish, and now the fetish had grown into a monstrous and crushing weight. It was as if the inspiration of their early years had left her heart to turn into a wall of silver bricks, erected by the silent work of evil spirits, between her and her husband. [N, 221]

In both cases the material interests, far from being humanized by their manipulators, have been the source of the dehumanization of those who have sought to possess them.

If the silver bricks form a wall between Mrs Gould and her husband, for Decoud they form the ballast that carries his body down to the bottom of the ocean, asserting crudely their primary materiality after controlling the lives of so many in rather different ways. Both Decoud and Nostromo are referred to as victims within the space of a page. Decoud is 'a victim of the disillusioned weariness which is the retribution meted out to intellectual audacity', while Nostromo is 'victim of the disenchanted vanity which is the reward of audacious action'. While Decoud finds that the man who attempts to live in a world of ideas is betrayed by that dumb matter which his ideas detach themselves from, Nostromo finds that audacious action has forced him to abandon first a woman, then a man, 'each in their last extremity', and that in so doing he has abandoned parts of himself. Conrad has earlier suggested:

> Action is consolatory. It is the enemy of thought and the friend of

flattering illusions. Only in the conduct of our action can we find the sense of mastery over the Fates. [N, 66][6]

But Nostromo's action has exacted such a price from him that it wearies him, for his action is not directed towards shared human ends, but towards the satisfaction of individual greed and the propitiation of inhuman material interests. Nostromo feels alienated, although he still has a sense of his own identity. Decoud, without either action or other people, loses his sense of self:

> [His individuality] had merged into the world of cloud and water, of natural forces and forms of nature. In our activity alone do we find the sustaining illusion of an independent existence as against the whole scheme of things of which we form a helpless part. [N, 497]

It is true that action alone does provide us with a sense of independent existence, but whether this is a 'sustaining illusion' is a moot point. There is certainly a lot of difference between Conrad's statement that we are a self-conscious part of nature – which he makes in his Author's Note to *The Shadow-Line* – and the suggestion that we form a helpless part of the whole scheme of things. Conrad seems here to be himself the victim of the disillusioned weariness which is the retribution meted out to intellectual audacity – or at least to the separation of the writer from audacious action. You cannot, as Conrad does here, assume that man is free to act and also assume that action prevents man from perceiving his essential unfreedom and helplessness.

This note of pessimistic determinism seems to me to express the contradictory outer limit of Conrad's vision in the novel. No English novel explores the relationship between material reality and human thought and history more searchingly than *Nostromo*, but his conviction that it is material interests rather than thought and ideas which govern history leads him to an assumption that human beings cannot therefore consciously change the world. The possibility of human beings changing their social relationships so as to alter their material interests in order to take their fates into their own hands is not one that he can entertain.

6 Yves Hervouet, *op. cit.*, suggests that this passage echoes lines in Anatole France's *L'Anneau d'Amethyste*.

4

The Secret Agent: animism and alienation

The first section of Geoffrey Hill's poem 'Annunciations' is directly concerned with the frightening portability of words about which I have already spoken, with their powerful but dangerous ability to shrug off their origins, their tendency to disclaim responsibility for their referents or effects and to assume an autonomy of which they are not ever possessed. Hill uses the social pretence that meat is similarly autonomous – displaced from fleshly origins – as a powerful symbol in his poem, and the symbol is disturbingly relevant to any discussion of *The Secret Agent*.

> The Word has been abroad, is back, with a tanned look
> From its subsistence in the stiffening-mire.
> Cleansing has become killing, the reward
> Touchable, overt, clean to the touch.
> Now at a distance from the steam of beasts,
> The loathly neckings and fat shook spawn
> (Each specimen-jar fed with delicate spawn)
> The searchers with the curers sit at meat
> And are satisfied. Such precious things put down
> And the flesh eased through turbulence the soul
> Purples itself; each eye squats full and mild
> While all who attend to fiddle or to harp
> For betterment, flavour their decent mouths
> With gobbets of the sweetest sacrifice.[1]

The 'half-ignorance' of the Belgian imperialists or of the 'grave and reverend persons' of *Nostromo* comes from being 'at a distance from the steam of beasts', or of human beings, and from the ability to manipulate people and things indirectly, through tokens, signs, words. In particular it is words which have this terrifying dual identity, subsiding in the stiffening-mire one minute, looking tanned and clean the next. The poem shows a concern at the potentiality for deception possessed by words, a concern for the way in which words can be used almost as hired

1 Geoffrey Hill, *King Log*. Deutsch, London, 1968, p. 14.

assassins – being sent out to do dirty work that their employer does not want to be involved in directly. As I have suggested before, such a concern goes along with the development of a society in which human relationships are indirect, in which words are used to do things to people, but indirectly. Just as it is easier to sign a death-warrant than actually to execute someone, so too it is easier to initiate certain actions through words, or even to talk about them, than to engage in them directly.

The Secret Agent is a novel obsessively concerned with such processes of indirect mediation. Conrad has dealt with this topic before, but in the context of imperialism, where the 'distance from the steam of beasts' is a geographical distance, a separation at once verbal and cultural. In *The Secret Agent* the setting is – in both senses of the word – domestic, and the word 'domestic' appears frequently in the pages of the novel. The earlier concern with the fact that a word could have one meaning in England and another meaning in South America, where it unleashed actions of which its originator was but half aware, is succeeded in this novel by a more horrified realization that geographical or cultural distance is not a necessary part of such ambiguous relations; between husband and wife the same knowing ignorance can subsist.

Hill's poem is particularly appropriate to *The Secret Agent* as it relates this view of the word as traveller in disguises to a comparable transformation of flesh to meat. The meat-eater does not think of the fleshly origins of what he or she is eating: appropriately we even use words to describe meat which do not remind us of the animal from which the meat has been obtained. Cooked meat is 'clean to the touch', whereas, for instance, raw liver is unpleasant to look at or to feel. Words too can be 'clean to the touch' even though they refer to, or initiate, very unclean actions. In *The Secret Agent* there are constant references to meat and to flesh, and their effect is to bring to our notice a characteristic reduction of the animate or living to the status of a thing. Alongside this is to be found a contrasting animism: objects not possessed of life are treated as if they were alive.[2]

Perhaps the most striking example of this sort of reversal in the novel comes when Inspector Heat looks at Stevie's fragmented remains, which are lying on a waterproof sheet spread over a table in the manner of a tablecloth, where they appear to be 'what might have been an accumulation of raw material for a cannibal feast' [SA, 86]; and Heat proceeds to peer

2 Yves Hervouet, *op. cit.*, notes interestingly, in a discussion of Conrad's debt to French, that this language's preference for certain forms inclines it to 'subjectivism and animism'.

at them with 'the slightly anxious attention of an indigent customer bending over what may be called the by-products of a butcher's shop with a view to an inexpensive Sunday dinner' [SA, 88].

I don't think that this sort of description is merely a gratuitous attempt to shock the reader, but a powerful symbol of a process which the novel presents as deeply embedded in the society with which it is concerned. The process is that of alienation, part of which involves the treatment of people as if they were merely things – not a direct treatment normally, but an indirect treatment through the manipulation of signs, or words. When Stevie's remains are regarded as if they were meat we are given a powerful, socially familiar symbol of the 'de-animation' of the living into lifeless objects, and the symbol illuminates a whole range of semi-human relationships in the novel. People throughout the novel treat other people as means to ends, as objects to be manipulated, rather than as fully human individuals. When Verloc eats the roast beef soon after Stevie's slaughter the point is made most explicitly: just as Verloc fails to associate the meat with Stevie's remains, so too he characteristically ignores the results of his actions, undertaking missions as though they were closed events, rather than ones which end in death for those he betrays. Stevie is blown into 'nameless fragments'; his depersonalization is ironically contrasted with the survival of the name written on his coat. The contrast can again be taken as a larger symbol of that portability of the word, which can survive the destruction of that to which it refers. Inspector Heat's greater interest in the named fragment of coat than the nameless fragments of Stevie is representative of his concern with tokens, clues, names, rather than with people.

I have already suggested that mirrored in this treatment of persons as things and things as living beings we can see a society which does in fact treat people as things, and which animates the dead matter around them. As Marx puts it, it is no longer the labourer who employs the means of production, but the means of production which employ the labourer. Robert Alter, in his book *Partial Magic*, comments on the same reversal of animate and inanimate in Dickens's work, and suggests that this 'weird displacement of animation' serves a realistic function of sorts because 'it reproduces the deformation of collective life, the reduction of individuals to instruments, in an acquisitive society that had scarcely begun to confront the grave problems of its own radical historical changes'.[3] 'Acquisitive society' is a bit

3 Robert Alter, *Partial Magic*. University of California Press, London, 1975, p. 96.

timid: what he means, or should mean, is capitalist society, and that same reversal can be seen wherever capitalism enters the arena of history. No novel of Dickens's presents us with this characteristic reversal more consistently or comprehensively than *The Secret Agent*. Not only are people treated as things (even a police constable is described 'as if he, too, were part of inorganic nature'), but objects start to assume a weird life of their own. A gentleman's coat texture has 'a character of elastic soundness, as if it were a living tissue'; the gas-jets in the Verloc's shop seem to have a life of their own; Mrs Neale is pictured as 'a sort of amphibious and domestic animal living in ashbins and dirty water', and the mechanical piano plays tunes without even the help of a piano stool.

Theodore Lidz, in his book *The Origin and Treatment of Schizophrenic Disorders*, notes that 'animism'; 'artificialism' (the belief that things are the product of human creation, rather than having their own creative activity), and 'participation' (the belief that behaviour influences inanimate nature as well as other people), are all stages through which, according to Piaget, children pass, but to which schizophrenics revert.[4] That we find such distortions of the relationship between the animate and the inanimate used symbolically by a writer such as Conrad suggests, I think, two things – firstly that there may be similarities between the social alienation of the *writer*, who is cut off from direct contact with people and who manipulates words not real events, and that of the mentally ill person who, for various reasons, is also cut off from sustaining human contact; secondly, and more importantly, that the writer in capitalist society can find socially available symbols of this isolation which express his or her situation in a way that is comprehensible and familiar to the reader who is neither a writer of fiction nor mentally ill. One has only to switch on the stock-market report on the radio with its absurd talk of 'rubbers held firm while metals showed some signs of insecurity' to realize that it is not just creative writers who see signs and things as possessed of an independent life of their own in our society.

Lidz makes the interesting point that there is a linguistic dimension to schizophrenic disorder. Not only does the schizophrenic lack those linguistic categories which allow him or her to filter sensory information and process it in an ordered way, but there is also a *semiotic* disruption: the schizophrenic confuses word with referent, partly reverting to that developmental stage described by Vygotsky in which the child sees the

4 Theodore Lidz, *The Origin and Treatment of Schizophrenic Disorders*. Hutchinson, London, 1975, p. 58.

word as attribute or property, rather than sign. Hill, in a comment on 'Annunciations' has noted:

> I suppose the impulse behind the work is an attempt to realize the jarring double-takes in words of common usage: as 'sacrifice' [section] (I) or 'Love' [section] (II) words which, like the word 'state', are assumed to have an autonomous meaning or value irrespective of context.[5]

In 'A Familiar Preface' to his *A Personal Record*, Conrad makes a statement on the 'force of words' which bears striking similarities to Hill's comment:

> You perceive the force of a word. He who wants to persuade should put his trust not in the right argument, but in the right word. The power of sound has always been greater than the power of sense. I don't say this by way of disparagement. It is better for mankind to be impressionable than reflective. Nothing humanely great – great, I mean, as affecting a whole mass of lives – has come from reflection. On the other hand, you cannot fail to see the power of mere words; such words as Glory, for instance, or Pity. . . . Give me the right word and the right accent and I will move the world. [APR, xi]

Hill's 'jarring double-takes' refer to that same verbal 'dual identity' as Conrad's distinction between sound and sense, or word and argument. Both are concerned with the double life that words can lead, and the betrayals that follow from this mode of existence. Both writers, too, perceive that this double identity is linked with larger duplicities, more far-reaching inhumanities. Verloc's domesticity appears 'clean to the touch', but is fuelled by and productive of that which is extremely unclean.

One of the key associations in *The Secret Agent* comes in the magnificently suggestive opening pages. The very deliberate parallel drawn between pornography and 'revolutionary' literature – the 'few books with titles hinting at impropriety' and the 'few apparently old copies of obscure newspapers, badly printed, with titles like the *Torch*, the *Gong* – rousing titles' – is very deliberate. Both share a common illusory reference to the real, saying the thing that is not, in Swift's ironic phrase. In a sense both offer their readers *fictions*, and the self-referential element in the novel which continues this parallel is to be found in the portrayal of Michaelis, the character who is writing a book, as the person most removed from actuality or a true knowledge of events. Michaelis talks to himself 'indifferent to the sympathy or hostility of his hearers'; he is no good in discussion,

5 Kenneth Allott (ed.), *The Penguin Book of Contemporary Verse*. Penguin, Harmondsworth, reprinted 1966, p. 391.

because the mere fact of hearing another voice disconcerted him painfully, confusing his thoughts at once – these thoughts that for so many years, in a mental solitude more barren than a waterless desert, no living voice had ever combatted, commented, or approved. [SA, 45]

His isolation of words from their life-giving contexts is on a par with the pornography and the 'revolutionary' literature, both of which are untested by any real, human scrutiny, by the pressure of reality. A theme that is to become crucial in *Under Western Eyes* is apparent here: direct contact with other people which is not cordoned off from the real world leads to true knowledge of self and others; isolation leads to a confusion of the real and the imaginary.

After his interview with Vladimir, Verloc is like a meat-eating man who is suddenly told that he must slaughter a cow, or like one used to gratifying himself with pornographic representations who is unexpectedly precipitated into the need to initiate a real sexual relationship. 'What is required at present is not writing, but the bringing to light of a distinct, significant fact.' Vladimir does not recognize the conventional division of labour between secret agent and agent provocateur; he insists upon a fact rather than a sign. Verloc is the archetypal shopkeeper, restricting his human contacts to the commercial and spuriously engaging. Conrad seems to make the association between his commercial activity, his domestic virtues and his spying explicit:

> The door of the shop was the only means of entrance to the house in which Mr Verloc carried on his business of a seller of shady wares, exercised his vocation of a protector of society, and cultivated his domestic virtues. [SA, 5]

Both his customers and the evening 'anarchist' visitors approach the shop with the collars of their overcoats turned up, a disguise later adopted by the Assistant Commissioner. All three aspects of Verloc's existence, then, represent three sides of the same triangle. All involve the detachment of something from full human intercourse or significance, treating it as independent, free-standing, apart.

Avrom Fleishman has chronicled and commented upon Conrad's repetitive use of the word 'secret' in *The Secret Agent*.[6] The world of *The Secret Agent* is a world of 'private individuals' who have the appearance of self-sufficiency and independence, but who are related to one another in all sorts of concealed but crucial ways. It is this privacy that, in part at least, explains the insistent reversal of animate and inanimate qualities in the novel. If it is contact with other human beings that makes us fully

6 Avrom Fleishman, *op. cit.*, p. 190 et seq.

human then the lack of such contact makes us, and others, appear to resemble things rather than human beings. And more than this: if people relate to one another through the medium of things, through commodities, then it is not surprising that these things should come to resemble people, and to assume a life of their own.

A society saturated with privacy and secrecy needs agents; a society which functions largely through agents and agencies becomes one of interconnected secrecies. Secrecy and agency belong to each other, and constitute together an interlocking unity which is part of the basic structure of capitalist society. There is an interesting shift in meaning of the word 'agency' towards the end of the seventeenth century; from meaning 'acting, action' in 1658, it comes to mean 'intermediation' in 1674, according to the Shorter Oxford dictionary. With the rise of capitalist social relations we see how the person who acts gives way in social significance to the person who performs the role of a go-between. Society is no longer largely based on direct relationships between people and people, or people and things, but on indirect relationships mediated through human and non-human channels.

With this change there is evidence of an accompanying change in the inner lives of individual human beings. Where society is based on the relationships of 'private' individuals, then almost inevitably a split arises between subjective experience and objective meaning, a split that I have suggested is an inbuilt potentiality in language itself, but which is exploited as never before in capitalist society. It has to be strongly stated that the distinction so common to us between private sensations and public behaviour is not an inevitable part of the human condition.

There are many examples of this dualism in *The Secret Agent*. Conrad's very ironic method rests on a revealed disjunction between private and public. It is because – with the exception of Stevie and the Professor, who are not treated ironically – no character testifies fully to his or her private feelings, that the narrative technique Conrad uses must go beyond public statements. The technique has to contrast what characters actually think, or what their motives really are, with what they say and do. It's not hard to see why dramatizations of the novel, even those written by Conrad himself, should have been so unsuccessful. An omniscient narrator is required if the total workings of a complex ensemble of social relations lacking a public determining centre of authority are to be uncovered. Irony depends upon a revealed contrast between intended and ex- pressed meaning, and thus Conrad's ironic method is perfectly suited to the treatment of a society in which private sensations and experiences, and public accountability and responsibility, are separated as a matter of deep principle. It is from the dominating distinction between exchange value and use value in capitalist society (if I may be excused recourse to Marxist jargon) that this distinction stems. The agent who is concerned only with what he can exchange his goods, rather than with what people will do with them, automatically thinks in terms of the public irrelevance of private feelings.

To describe such a society the novelist is driven to use a more universal ironic method, one which actually enacts the distinction between what is said and what is meant. A society not divided in this fundamental way possesses, as it were, a single linguistic currency: words may go abroad, but their exchange rate is the same there as here. In the sort of society depicted in *The Secret Agent* words start to lose this single identity: like commodities they start to be possessed of an exchange value and a use value. Indeed, to refer again to Conrad's bête noir, in certain circumstances words are literally commodities: even by the late eighteenth century literary hacks were being paid by the word for work completed, and the journalist is the contemporary example par excellence for Conrad of one who deals with words as objects rather than as meaning. Conrad's ironic method succeeds in enacting this distinction between what is said and what is meant by forcing the reader continually to examine statements made by characters in two contexts – that of the character's utterance and discourse as he or she sees it, and that of the author's ironic consideration of it. In his Author's Note to the novel Conrad makes it clear that the artistic purpose of using an ironic method was deliberate, as he believed that 'ironic treatment alone would enable me to say all I felt I would have to say in scorn as well as in pity'. The technique constantly juxtaposes what I do think it is not too fanciful to describe as the exchange value and the use value of words – the immediate role they play publicly, and their deeper significance either in the inner life of a character, or in their wider, and ignored, meaning.[7] Apart from Stevie and the Professor, no character in the novel habitually says what he or she is actually thinking. Indeed, the

7 Compare the following statement by A. A. Leont'ev:
'In a class society (and most clearly in capitalist societies) the objective meaning of a referent (or a word) and its sense diverge permanently because the 'personal' interests, 'personal' motives are divergent from the interests of society as a whole.' 'Sense as a Psychological Concept'. In Jan Průcha (ed.), *Soviet Studies in Language and Language Behavior*, North-Holland, Amsterdam and London, 1976, p. 87.

only time that Verloc speaks sincerely, the result is not what he expects.

Conrad actually seems to use a sort of parodic newspaper style at times in order to effect his ironic purpose. Consider, for example, the opening of the twelth chapter in the book.

> Winnie Verloc, the widow of Mr Verloc, the sister of the late faithful Stevie (blown to fragments in a state of innocence and in the conviction of being engaged in a humanitarian enterprise), did not run beyond the door of the parlour. [SA, 266]

Winnie is described here in the neutral informative phrases of the journalist, and the matter-of-factness of this description is of course belied by the reader's knowledge of the fact that her inner world is in complete turmoil. A layer of comfortable words lies over this fact, and because there is this gap between the words and the reality, the reader is made aware of the narrator's desperate sadness at the human isolation of Winnie which is symbolically portrayed in the isolation of her feelings from the 'public' language used to describe her. Except ironically, no one who felt for Winnie could describe her in these terms.

Conrad uses this technique, and variants of it, very frequently. In his introduction to Thomas Beer's study of Stephen Crane, he recounts how he used playfully to taunt Crane with a phrase ('barbarously abrupt') taken from Crane's writing. The same technique occurs at the start of the tale *Because of the Dollars:* the narrator has heard a person described as 'a really *good* man'.

> I turned round at once to look at the phenomenon. The 'really *good* man' had a very broad back. [WTT, 169]

The technique is to take a word or phrase out of the context of an utterance and to use it as a name. It draws attention to the words used, giving them a spurious freedom from context. Our attention is thus focused on the way in which words can be transported, can be taken out of context, and the gap between the (in this case) person described and the words used is highlighted.

Conrad also makes use of what has been called free indirect speech,[8] in which the characteristics of direct and indirect speech are mixed so as to confuse narrative viewpoint with the viewpoint of the character concerned. However, whereas a writer such as Virginia Woolf will use this technique to 'get inside' a character, Conrad uses it to focus attention on to the difference between the narrative viewpoint and the character's view of things. A

8 For an interesting discussion of this (which unfortunately does not refer to Conrad) see Roy Pascal, *The Dual Voice.* Manchester University Press, Manchester, 1977.

good example of this comes at the beginning of the tale *The End of the Tether*, where we are taken into Captain Whalley's thoughts at the same time as we are forced to look at them 'from the outside':

> There had been a time when men counted: there were not so many carriages in the colony then, though Mr Denham, he fancies, had a buggy. [TEOTT, 194]

That 'fancies', coming where we are expecting 'fancied', suddenly takes us out of Captain Whalley's consciousness into an external point of view from which Captain Whalley seems smaller, more pathetic, than he had before. The technique surfaces time and time again in *The Secret Agent* to draw attention to the limitations of a character's self-knowledge or self-awareness. Take the following passage:

> For he was difficult to dispose of, that boy. He was delicate and, in a frail way, good-looking, too, except for the vacant droop of his lower lip. Under our excellent system of compulsory education he had learned to read and write, notwithstanding the unfavourable aspect of the lower lip. [SA, 8]

We move here from prose which clearly mirrors the thought patterns and sequences of Winnie, to narrative interjections from a different perspective which comment upon these thought patterns and sequences. Winnie would not describe Stevie's gape in the way it is described here. The technique of starting a paragraph with 'For' is a much favoured one of Virginia Woolf's, and she uses it in a similar way to move from narrative viewpoints into those of a particular character, although in her writings the transition is often impossible to pin-point precisely.

Near the start of the novel there is a revealing description of the way in which Winnie's mother's delicacy in choosing 'the least valuable and most dilapidated articles' to take with her when she moves out passed unacknowledged because

> Winnie's philosophy consisted in not taking notice of the inside of facts; she assumed that mother took what suited her best. As to Mr Verloc, his intense meditation, like a sort of Chinese wall, isolated him completely from the phenomena of this world of vain effort and illusory appearances. [SA, 154]

'Not taking notice of the inside of facts' is a habit of which many of the characters in *The Secret Agent* are possessed, and it extends to their use of language. Winnie treats words in terms of their outer significance, their exchange value – until, that is, events force her to do otherwise. Conrad's technique is to draw attention to the 'inside' of the words she uses, the hidden meanings which she habitually ignores.

Far from constituting a special political target, the 'anarchists' in *The Secret Agent* are in effect treated as *symptomatic* of the society in which they are resident, rather than as worrying *exceptions* to its norms. Conrad's criticism of them is not materially different from his criticism of the Verlocs, or of Sir Ethelred. It is not primarily a political criticism. Conrad's disapproval of socialist and anarchist ideas is well known, but *The Secret Agent* is not in any way a crude piece of Conservative propaganda. In a letter to William Blackwood, written on 29 October 1897, Conrad takes exception to a phrase in a review of Hallam Tennyson's *Memoir* of his father. The phrase, 'a dirty rascal had only to wave a cap of liberty upon a pike to enlist the enthusiasm of hundreds of educated young gentleman', rouses Conrad to object:

> Not every man who 'waved a cap of liberty on a pike' was a scoundrel. And England had not only given refuge to criminals. There was a greatness in that mistaken hospitality which is the inheritance of all parties. Of course I do not defend political crime. It is repulsive to me by tradition, by sentiment, and even by reflexion. But some of their men had struggled for an idea, openly, in the light of day, and sacrificed to it all that to most men makes life worth living. [LBM, 14]

Perhaps the two important words here are 'idea' and 'openly'; the 'anarchists' in *The Secret Agent* have few ideas, and they do not struggle openly. Their secrecy is representative of a fundamental duplicity, involving themselves as well as other people, which is not limited to them in the novel. They do, however, offer the most striking symbol in the novel of that separation of private from public that is the focus of Conrad's deepest enquiry. In his Author's Note to the novel Conrad attacks the actual perpetrators of the Greenwich Observatory explosion who had blown a man to bits, 'for nothing even most remotely resembling an idea, anarchistic or otherwise'.

To struggle *openly* for an *idea* is to link private and public, to attempt to unite that which is subjectively human with that which is objectively human. Even if such a struggle is mistaken, it is mistaken honestly. The 'anarchists' in *The Secret Agent* have few ideas, and those they do have they do not struggle for openly; it is worth pointing out that the criticism made of Verloc by Vladimir is the same as that made of his fellow conspirators by the Professor – they talk but do not act. In a letter written to Cunninghame Graham on 7 October 1907, Conrad stresses the important distinction between the 'shams' and the sincere:

> But I don't think that I've been satirizing the revolutionary world. All these people are not revolutionaries – they are Shams. And as

regards the Professor I did not intend to make him despicable. He is incorruptible at any rate. In making him say 'madness and despair – give me that for a lever and I will move the world' I wanted to give him a note of perfect sincerity. At the worst he is a megalomaniac of an extreme type. And every extremist is respectable. [LCG, 170]

Conrad adds, shortly after, the comment:

By Jove! If I had the necessary talent I would like to go for the true anarchist – which is the millionaire. Then you would see the venom flow. But it's too big a job. [LCG, 170]

By 'respectable' I take it that Conrad means 'worthy of respect', rather than 'a respectable member of society'. The Professor is worthy of respect because of his sincerity, because what he believes, what he says, and what he does are the same. It is a measure of the society with which Conrad is concerned that the two most completely sincere characters in the novel are the Professor and Stevie – a megalomaniac and a half-wit. Inspector Heat's grudging respect for ordinary thieves may relate to a recognition that there is, too, a sort of sincerity in their lives: they do not pretend to be anything other than what they are, and what they are they express in action. We can recall Conrad's own respect for the stone-breaking convicts of Dartmoor.

Similarities between the Verlocs, the anarchists and others are manifest in their common mistreatment of language. Verloc, for example, quite naturally distinguishes between what he actually thinks and what he says: that is what a secret agent has to do.

'With a voice like that,' he said, putting on the husky conversational pedal, 'I was naturally trusted. And I knew what to say, too.'
Mr Vladimir, arranging his cravat, observed him in the glass over the mantelpiece.
'I daresay you have the social revolutionary jargon by heart well enough,' he said, contemptuously. 'Vox et. . . . You haven't ever studied Latin – have you?' [SA, 24]

A large family of people whose members 'know what to say' lives within Conrad's novels, and in each case this knowledge involves manipulating language to influence other people, rather than honestly to express an inner conviction or to communicate a sincere belief. Although Vladimir goes on to sneer at Verloc's anarchist friends who are, he says, capable of writing 'a *charabia* every bit as incomprehensible as Chinese', his own speech is dotted with foreign words like 'charabia' and as Verloc is made to realize, is indicative of his own lack of real understanding of the anarchists and their movements. Vladimir's fluency is comparable to the fluency of Michaelis, the man who cannot *talk* coherently to another person, but who, according to Ossipon, can be relied upon to give a speech dissociating the anarchists from the bomb outrage. Without any sense of self mockery, Ossipon points out:

> What he would say would be utter bosh, but he has a turn of talk that makes it go down all the same. [SA, 78]

Doubtless it is this that endears him to the radical chic bourgeoisie amongst whom he moves: he uses exciting words, but they know (or think they know) that the words are safe.

Conrad is not so sure, it would appear, that they are safe. However still-born a word may be – whether it is the squawk of a parrot or the bosh talked by Michaelis – it can still spring to life in most unexpected ways. I have already pointed out that Conrad on more than one occasion compares words to bullets. In a letter to Edward Garnett he uses a significant variant of this comparison.

> If you mean to say that you do not make yourself understood by me it's an odious libel on both of us. Where do you think the illumination – the short and vivid flash of which I have been boasting to you came from? Why! From your words, words, words. They exploded like stored powder barrels – while another man's words would have fizzled out in speaking and left darkness unrelieved by a forgotten spurt of futile sparks. An explosion is the most lasting thing in the universe. It leaves disorder, remembrance, room to move, a clear space. Ask your Nihilist friends. [LFC, 79]

It is true that Conrad distinguishes between Garnett's well chosen and, we presume, sincere words, and the words of 'another man'. But in spite of this the image of the explosion is a telling one which points to Conrad's awareness of the stored potentiality in even a carelessly used word. The link made here between 'exploding words' and real explosions is also made forcibly in Conrad's tale *The Informer*. The informer of the story is loved by a woman who, we are told, 'knew little of anything except of words', and who is in an odd way as incapable of scrutinizing herself as is Singleton. 'X' says of her:

> I imagine that this charming, generous, and independent creature had never known in her life a single genuine thought; I mean a single thought detached from small human vanities, or whose source was not in some conventional perception. [SOS, 92]

X, the anarchist, telling the narrator his story, understands the fascination that the informer of the story has for this woman, as he has experienced a comparable prestige among the 'well fed bourgeoisie' who have bought thousands of copies of his pamphlets. He rhetorically demands of the narrator of the tale whether he does not know

> that an idle and selfish class loves to see mischief being made, even if it is made at its own expense? Its own life being all a matter of pose and gesture, it is unable to realize the power and the danger of a real movement and of words that have no sham meaning. It is all fun and sentiment. [sos, 78][9]

An aspect of *The Secret Agent* that is often ignored is Conrad's criticism of 'an idle and selfish class', which is as sharp and as telling as is his criticism of the anarchists. Few people *work* in any real way in the novel, and it is not just the radical chic drawing room into which the Assistant Commissioner enters, and in which he finds Michaelis and his lady benefactor, where the idle rich are condemned. Consider, for instance, this passage from early on in *The Secret Agent*:

> [Mr Verloc] surveyed through the park railings the evidences of the town's opulence and luxury with an approving eye. All these people had to be protected. Protection is the first necessity of opulence and luxury. They had to be protected; and their horses, carriages, houses, servants had to be protected; and the source of their wealth had to be protected in the heart of the city and the heart of the country; the whole social order favourable to their hygienic idleness had to be protected against the shallow enviousness of unhygienic labour. [sa, 12]

The fact that this speech is given, implicitly, to Verloc should guard us against in any way assuming that its sentiments are presented for approval, and if this were not enough then Conrad's totally consistent attitude to the moral centrality of work should convince us that the whole social order Verloc wishes to protect is one about which Conrad himself has very mixed feelings. We can remember that the idle Ossipon also gives lectures on the socialistic aspects of hygiene, and this word assumes what Conrad appears to find a rather nasty set of connotations – including that, I think, of contraception – in the novel. There is an essential privacy in hygiene: for all its positive features, Conrad uses it here as a symbol of the separation of things from their life-giving contacts. It is certainly true that an obsession with hygiene does seem to accompany a bourgeois emphasis on privacy and self-containedness. I would not wish to put forward a case for dirt, but I do think that an obsession with dirt is a reflection of an obsessive need to draw boundaries round the self, to define the self in terms of separation from, rather than contact with, other things and other people. The great thing

9 My attention was drawn to the relevance of these two quotations from *The Informer* by a reading of Avrom Fleishman's chapter on *The Secret Agent*.

about money in a capitalist society is that it doesn't reveal the secrets of its origins: as Herbert Pocket points out in *Great Expectations*, a gentleman may not keep a pub, but a pub may keep a gentleman. 'Hygiene', therefore, reflects the atomistic nature of capitalist society – a society in which money can appear detached from its origins, in which people can live in an opulence protected from the unhygienic labour which produces that opulence.[10]

At the start of the second chapter of the novel there is an apparently isolated reference to 'here and there a victoria with the skin of some wild beast inside and a woman's face and hat emerging above the folded hood'. The privacy of the coach separates its passenger from social realities in much the same way that the animal skin is removed from its savage origins, and both stand as potent symbols of the hygienic idleness of the rich. The reference chimes in with a similar one placed near the beginning of *Under Western Eyes*:

> He noted ... the sidelong, brilliant glance of a pretty woman – with a delicate head, and covered in the hairy skins of wild beasts down to her feet, like a frail and beautiful savage. [UWE, 40]

Characters in *The Secret Agent* treat words much as these women treat the skins of savage beasts, as pretty things which can be played with. They forget where they have come from and what they represent. Karl Yundt can talk about 'red-hot applications on their vile skins – hey? Can't you smell and hear from here the thick hide of the people burn and sizzle', but it is obvious that to him (although not to Stevie) these are just words.

Just as Vladimir's ill-considered words turn into bloody deeds through the intermediation of his agent, so the words of the Professor strike Inspector Heat with their 'atrocious allusiveness'. Heat has just seen the fragmented flesh of Stevie, and the Professor's words have the effect of unlocking a freshly perceived reality in Heat's memory. A word may be unconsidered, just as Winnie's stabbing of Verloc is to her 'only a blow', but it has the potentiality to release undreamed of consequences, like stored powder barrels.

In an interesting essay entitled 'On the Margins of Discourse', Barbara Herrnstein Smith considers a topic about which Conrad has strong feelings – what she calls 'prefabricated discourse or utterance'. As an example of what she means she refers to the messages in greeting-cards:

---

10 Conrad's use of the word 'hygiene' here has interesting similarities to Sylvia Plath's use of the word 'pure' in many of her poems.

Greeting-card messages are not poems. What they are is something we may call *prefabricated* utterances: verbal structures preassembled for later use as natural utterances. Indeed, it is precisely because the greeting-card message must meet the expressive needs of so many people that its language is so vague and general.[11]

The person who designs and prints a card with 'Happy Birthday' on it need feel no desire to wish anyone a happy birthday: the words may be, almost certainly are, merely tokens to be manipulated. The designer's attitude to the words is comparable to the farmer's attitude to the food he or she produces; the farmer doesn't have to feel hungry, or to feel that the food looks appetizing. (I should add that my earlier points about the sort of society with which one is concerned are valid here: without indulging in ahistorical dreams about 'organic communities', one can argue that in certain societies things are treated more as use-values than as exchange-values.)

Conrad is deeply suspicious of prefabricated utterance, but at the same time he recognizes that prefabricated utterances can 'explode like stored powder barrels'. When Vladimir is considering the sort of outrage that needs to be committed to force the British to act against those anarchists in their midst, he argues against a murderous attack on a theatre or a restaurant:

> [These would suffer from] the suggestion of non-political passion; the exasperation of a hungry man, an act of social revenge. All this is used up; it is no longer instructive as an object lesson in revolutionary anarchism. *Every newspaper has ready-made phrases to explain such manifestations away.* [SA, 32; my italics]

I don't know to what extent Conrad realized that this was literally true: newspapers have headlines made up waiting for events to take place which 'fit' them – words waiting for reality to catch up with them. There is a case to be made for prefabricated utterance of course: I do not feel insulted or slighted when I receive a pre-printed birthday card, nor do I feel that the message, because it predates the intention of the sender of the card, is somehow insincere or impersonal. But I do think that Conrad is right to see this sort of prefabrication (which needn't be written, as we will see) as a symptom of a larger anonymity in the mediating networks of communication in the Britain of his – and our – day.

What I think can be said is that when the reliance on prefabrications reaches a certain level, then we find that just as the machine starts to operate the man or woman rather than vice-

11 Barbara Herrnstein Smith, 'On the Margins of Discourse'. *Critical Analysis*, June 1975, I 4, p. 784.

versa, so too language can become an alienated part of human beings which instead of expressing their needs and relationships, uses them to express its dehumanized self. The parallel with machinery is not I hope a glib one. The person who gets his or her opinions in the form of prefabricated phrases from the popular press is in a real sense dehumanized, operated as a ventriloquist's dummy by other people's insincere words. Winnie Verloc, for instance, is a woman whose life is impoverished because she lacks the words that could bring to her the richness of her social heritage as a member of a particular linguistic community; she was 'a woman of singularly few words, either for public or private use'. Her philosophy of not taking notice of the inside of facts is a philosophy of treating the world as a world of exchange values, in which the only really human centre is herself and her relationship with Stevie. In her misery at the end of the novel, searching for some human warmth and solidarity, she has to have recourse to something like a greeting-card message:

> As often happens in the lament of poor humanity rich in suffering but indigent in words, the truth – the very cry of truth – was found in a worn and artificial shape picked up somewhere among the phrases of sham sentiment. [SA, 298]

The statement is sensitively balanced between a recognition that Winnie can discover some means to express her genuine humanity in the worn phrase, and the saddened implication that this somehow testifies to a fundamental impoverishment in her life.

When Ossipon meets the Professor immediately after the bombing their conversation leads at one point to an argument about language and the meaning of words. Ossipon has described the bomb outrage as 'criminal', meaning that it will bring problems for the anarchist groups. The Professor takes him up on his use of this word:

> The little man lifted his thin black eyebrows with dispassionate scorn.
> 'Criminal! What is that? What *is* crime? What can be the meaning of such an assertion?'
> 'How am I to express myself? One must use the current words,' said Ossipon, impatiently. [SA, 71]

That is exactly, Conrad seems to be saying, what one must not do. We can see how Conrad manages here to give the Professor 'the note of perfect sincerity'; for the perfectly sincere person, that is, the person who wants words to mean the same to other people as they mean to him or her, to abolish the difference between their use value and their exchange value, does *not* 'use the current words'. Using the current words is using other people's words, words which may even be 'prefabricated' and behind which no felt intention may reside at all. The Professor may be 'a pest in a street full of men', but he is 'perfectly sincere', he knows the realities from which the words he uses emerge and to which they refer. Ossipon, in contrast, indulges in sexual liaisons the note of which used to be 'an unbounded trustfulness in the language of sentiment and manly tenderness', although his shock at Winnie's suicide seems to have destroyed this trustfulness by the end of the novel.

Winnie and Ossipon both use words carelessly and un-thinkingly – as carelessly stored powder barrels. Both are surprised, in different ways, when explosions of meaning take place. Ossipon cannot get the journalistic phrases of the newspaper report out of his head, although clearly the newspaper copy-writer has not been at all bothered by the implications of the preformed phrases he is using. Winnie too is struck by the 'atrocious allusiveness' of the words: 'The drop given was fourteen feet.' In a deliberately ambiguous passage, Conrad makes it very clear what he thinks of newspapers – playing on the reader's memory of the phrase 'the gutter press':

> In front of the great doorway a dismal row of newspaper sellers standing clear of the pavement dealt out their wares from the gutter. It was a raw, gloomy day of the early spring; and the grimy sky, the mud of the streets, the rags of the dirty men harmonized excellently with the eruption of the damp, rubbishy sheets of paper soiled with printers' ink. The posters, maculated with filth, garnished like tapestry the sweep of the curbstone. [SA, 79]

The filth too, could be literal or metaphorical – mud from the streets or advertisement for the filthy content of the papers. As Conrad adds, a line further on: 'The effect was of indifference, of a disregarded distribution.' The indifference of the men to their wares chimes in with the indifference of the journalist to the events his words describe: the whole scene paints a chilling picture of the discreteness of a particular link in a chain of communication. The newspaper sellers are like the pilgrims in *Heart of Darkness*, squirting bullets into the river bank oblivious to what effect they are having. When meaning becomes objecti-fied and treated as a commodity, then instead of being that which unites human beings, something discovered collectively through work, it is something that can be used to divide them.

Stevie, like the Professor, does not treat words in this way. His moral superiority is associated with a lack of linguistic skill:

> [Stevie] was no master of phrases, and perhaps for that very reason his thoughts lacked clearness and precision. But he felt with greater completeness and some profundity. [SA, 171]

Like 'poor humanity', he is 'rich in suffering but indigent in words', and the completeness and profundity of his feelings are connected with his inability to manipulate words as arbitrary signs. Words, for Stevie, are directly evocative of particular realities. Explaining to Verloc why Stevie has got so worked up after listening to the anarchists' gory figures of speech, Winnie explains:

> 'He isn't fit to hear what's said here. He believes it's all true. He knows no better. He gets into his passions over it.' [SA, 59]

The word never comes back with a tanned look for Stevie – it takes him straight into the stiffening-mire:

> The mere names of certain transgressions filled him with horror. He had been always easily impressed by speeches. [SA, 173]

Arriving at an *idea*, involving abstraction, is for him extremely difficult:

> Now he went along without pride, shamblingly, and muttering half words, and even words that would have been whole if they had not been made up of halves that did not belong to each other. It was as though he had been trying to fit all the words he could remember to his sentiments in order to get some sort of corresponding idea. And, as a matter of fact, he got it at last. He hung back to utter it at once.
> 'Bad world for poor people.' [SA, 171]

Stevie is still at that stage of cognitive development which A.R. Luria has described as 'situational' or 'graphic' rather than 'conceptual'.[12] He thinks in purely concrete terms most of the time; he cannot without great difficulty abstract conceptual principles from his concrete experience.

At a later stage in the novel we learn that what is humanly important for Winnie is apprehended not verbally but graphically. After she has learned of Stevie's death, Verloc's words to her lose all meaning and semiotic identity, becoming, as Conrad ironically describes them, 'waves of air of the proper length, propagated in accordance with correct mathematical formulas'. But her thoughts fly to the reality of Stevie's poor, smashed body without the aid of words:

> A park! That's where the boy was killed. A park – smashed branches, torn leaves, gravel, bits of brotherly flesh and bone, all spouting up

---

12 A. R. Luria, *Cognitive Development: its Cultural and Social Foundations.* Harvard University Press, London, 1976, p. 162.

together in the manner of a firework. She remembered now what she had heard, *and she remembered it pictorially.* [SA, 260; my italics]

She uses two sorts of thinking – one predominantly verbal, for her 'official' dealings, including those with Verloc, and one predominantly graphic or pictorial, for her human relationships with, above all, Stevie.

These two types of thinking, Luria argues, are very different:

> [Graphic methods of generalization] are based on an individual's practical experience, whereas at the core of 'conceptual' or 'categorical' thinking is the shared experience of society conveyed through its linguistic system. This reliance on society-wide criteria transforms graphic thinking processes into a scheme of semantic and logical operations in which words become the principal tool for abstraction and generalization.[13]

Stevie's thoughts are seemingly 'fitted into' words, rather than conducted through the medium of words. Stevie reacts so strongly to the cabman's beating of his horse not because he believes in the abstract that it is wrong, but because he

> knew what it was to be beaten. He knew it from experience. [SA, 171]

Stevie, unlike Ossipon, has no trustfulness in the language of manly sentiment: he trusts his concrete experiences only, and words have meaning to him purely in terms of their ability to evoke memories of such concrete experiences, whether such an evocation has been intended or not.

He is thus capable of illustrating the duplicity involved in the manipulating of abstractions and generalization by other characters in the novel. Told that Mr Verloc is a good man, it never occurs to him that this could just be a phrase tossed out to keep him quiet. Luria claims that through language human beings can create 'objective logical codes' which enable a person to go beyond direct experience and to draw conclusions that have the same objectivity as the data of direct sensory experience.[14] I agree that abstraction and generalization allow human beings to go beyond direct experience, but not that they have the same objectivity as the data of direct sensory experience. We see that Stevie cannot go beyond personal experience, he cannot arrive at abstractions – but because of this he cannot make the sort of mistake that Winnie makes. He knows what words mean in really human terms. He does, however, make a different sort of mistake: although he never detaches words from their referents, he fails to understand that other people do. Quite

13 Luria, *op. cit.*, p. 52.
14 Luria, *op. cit.*, p. 10.

simply, he cannot understand that people can tell lies. The assumption that 'society-wide criteria' are necessarily reliable ignores the problems created by a divided society, in which words have a complex identity which reflects the divisions of society.

Stevie, unlike his sister, who puts her trust in face values, wishes 'to go to the bottom of the matter'. He is unwilling to accept words at their market quotation (what an appropriate phrase, again, 'face value' is here!), but wants to cash them into a more immediately human currency. It is superbly ironic that Winnie should put her trust in face values when we have seen how wide is the gap between the face she herself puts on for her customers and her inner feelings. More than once her face is described as a mask – a mask which, by the end of the novel, she wishes to tear off. Just as her shop has a commercial front and a domestic interior, so she has a public face and a private identity. But she does not realize until the end of the novel that the words which she takes at their face value have also a hidden human significance. 'The drop given was fourteen feet' is not just a journalistic phrase: it refers to an appalling reality.

One of the profoundest ironies in this most ironical of novels is that the one time Verloc speaks to her in perfect sincerity she disregards his words. He too makes the mistake of believing that he is taken at his own valuation of himself, whereas he is loved not for himself but as a means to a desired end.

> The self-confident tone grew upon Mrs Verloc's ear which let most of the words go by; for what were words to her now? What could words do to her for good or evil in the face of her fixed idea? [SA, 250]

Verloc commented to Vladimir that his voice led people to trust him, and this commitment to insincerity finally betrays him into a fatal reliance on its persuasive powers. After his own death, his widow is in her turn betrayed by an ill-chosen reliance on the words of Ossipon. Language, it would seem, is not mocked.

If Stevie's imprisonment in the concrete has the effect of exposing the duplicity of those capable of manipulating words in a more detached way, it does not really offer the reader anything like a feasible solution to the problems raised by the suscepti-bility of words to misuse. The character who does offer us some hope is the Assistant Commissioner. We have been told that his preference for a post of colonial administration rather than a desk job in England was based on a feeling that the latter had a 'confined nature' and an 'apparent lack of reality'. Not only does this bear witness to Conrad's feeling that British coloni-alism was to be distinguished from others, it also presents the Assistant Commissioner as a man who prefers to see the reality rather than to manipulate the symbol. He is at once aware of the need for abstractions and also of their potentiality for betrayal:

> 'Here I am stuck in a litter of paper,' he reflected, with unreasonable resentment, 'supposed to hold all the threads in my hands, and yet I can but hold what is put in my hand, and nothing else. And they can fasten the other ends of the threads where they please.' [SA, 115]

When we recall that it is words about which he is speaking the passage is very revealing. By leaving his office and his official routine, the Assistant Commissioner is able to check where the other ends of the threads are in fact attached. He mistrusts words, but knows that they have to be used. If they have to be used, however, he will take the greatest care to ensure that they are not being misused. In this respect he is not so dissimilar to Joseph Conrad.

5

Fiction and truth

In *The Secret Agent* the Assistant Commissioner, worried about
not knowing where the 'other ends of the threads' are being
attached, takes steps to find this out. He thus avoids both the
perils of over-abstraction of the 'anarchists', and also the limitations of Stevie's imprisonment in concrete experience. If this
is Conrad's practical solution to the problems of words, what
implications does it have for the reader of novels? Are the 'ends
of the threads' attached anywhere at all? How is the reader to
test the truth or otherwise of what he or she reads? Conrad
certainly seems to have believed that it was not nonsensical to
talk of fiction conveying or containing some sort of truth. In
his essay 'Books', he suggests that 'some sort of truth' can be
found 'at the heart of fiction', although in the essay 'Travel' he
talks of the romancing of the writer of fiction, and suggests
perhaps half ironically that the truth in him is disguised in
various garments, from gold mantles to rags. These are probably
far from being well thought-out or considered critical
judgements, but Conrad does use the words 'truth' and 'lying'
in conjunction with discussions of his novels frequently enough
to suggest that there was a problem for him here.

I have suggested that at certain times – the passage describing
Chester and his 'antique' companion in *Lord Jim*, for example –
Conrad appears to be writing about the experience of writing. I
have quoted from his Author's Note to *The Shadow-Line* to the
effect that 'whatever falls under the dominion of our senses' must
be in nature, and cannot differ in its essence from 'all the other
effects of the visible and tangible world of which we are a
self-conscious part'. However, I have also referred to his
description of the writing of *Nostromo* 'away from the world',
but fully engaged with the might of his Creator, 'wrestling with
the Lord'. The question that presents itself is: 'What is the
relationship between 'the visible and tangible world' and the
'handful of pages that the writer of fiction manages eventually
to produce'?

Referring to 'Chester and his antique partner' in *Lord Jim*, Marlow/Conrad dismissed them for being 'too phantasmal', adding that 'a word carries far.' The 'phantasmal' nature of literary characters seems to have been a constant concern of Conrad's – not that they necessarily appeared so in the writing, but that reduced to a handful of pages when the novel was complete they seemed very insubstantial. The effort of writing *Nostromo* was comparable to a winter passage westward round Cape Horn – but the results less tangible. Writing (in French) to Marguerite Poradowska on 24 April 1894, Conrad described finishing *Almayer's Folly* in the following terms:

> It's finished! A scratch of the pen writing 'The End', and suddenly that whole company of people who have spoken in my ear, moved before my eyes, lived with me for so many years, becomes a troop of phantoms, who are withdrawing, growing dim, and merging – indistinct and pallid – with the sunlight of this brilliant and sombre day. [LJCMP, 66]

The literary character seems to reduce into a hallucination or a phantom 'outside of the work'. What truth can come from such illusory creations?

Although, as Norman Sherry has adequately demonstrated, Conrad drew on his actual experiences and on the real world quite directly for his fiction, it is not true to say, as does David Thorburn in his *Conrad's Romanticism*, that Conrad was 'in thrall to a narrowly literal conception of fiction',[1] although Thorburn quite rightly points out that Conrad admitted that his capacities for invention were dramatically circumscribed. But Conrad wrote to Marguerite Poradowska, of *The Secret Agent*:

> anarchy and anarchists are outside my experience; I know almost nothing of the philosophy, and nothing at all of the men. I created this out of whole cloth. [LJCMP, 116]

Jessie Conrad also recounts a relevant anecdote in her *Joseph Conrad and his Circle*:

> I remember bitterly reproaching my husband for not having ever spoken of this episode [*The Secret Sharer*] to me before he wrote the story. He gave a hoot of delight, and then as soon as he recovered from his unusual outburst of mirth, gave me a great hug and explained: 'My dear, it is pure fiction. I don't know where the idea came from, but I've taken you in beautifully. Hurrah.'[2]

1 David Thorburn, *op. cit.*, p. 57.
2 Jessie Conrad, *Joseph Conrad and his Circle*. Jarrolds, London, 1935, p. 77.

It seems that it is Jessie, rather than her husband, who has the narrowly literal conception of fiction here – as well as a rather placid view of the possibility of his having harboured a fugitive killer. Conrad appears to use the word 'fiction' (if Jessie's report is accurate) to mean 'not relating to an actual occurrence' as well as, possibly, 'creative writing unsullied by borrowings from actual experience'. The phrase 'taken you in beautifully' is oddly reminiscent of deceit rather than creativity.

Thorburn's suggestion has also to be set against the fact that although Conrad did admit that he couldn't 'invent', he did not use the 'raw material' of his experience in an untreated form. Conrad once wrote to Bennett (on 10 March 1902):

> You stop just short of being absolutely real because you are faithful to your dogmas of realism. Now realism in art will never approach reality.
> [JCLL I, 303]

The job of the writer is not to be a photographer in words, reproducing particular sensations and impressions as accurately as possible. Bennett's naturalism does not seem to have been profound enough for Conrad; profundity was not a matter of *reproducing* something exactly, but of going further into it, explaining it. Marlow does not just want to reproduce his experiences in his listeners: not only does he admit that that would be impossible, but he also admits that they see *more* than he did then.

Conrad does seem to have seen his function as a writer to have been that of extracting something from experience. Writing to Sir Sidney Colvin on 18 March 1917, he noted that although he had been called a writer of the sea, of the tropics, a descriptive writer, a romantic writer, and also a realist, 'as a matter of fact all my concern has been with the 'ideal' value of things, events and people' [JCLL II, 303]. The statement is by no means totally clear; it's certainly not the case that Conrad in his works looks for ideal truths which exist independent of context, either in people or in events. None of the characters in *The Secret Agent*, for example, can really be considered as a fixed, autonomous 'character', independent of time and place. Their interrelations one with another and with the larger social and natural world are seen to be inseparable from what they are. But Conrad does obviously try as a writer to abstract some generalized truths from the 'facts' on which he bases his novels. He took Richard Curle severely to task for trying to fill in biographical details to supplement what was printed in his novels:

> Didn't it ever occur to you, my dear Curle, that I knew what I was doing in leaving the facts of my life and even of my tales in the back-

ground? Explicitness, my dear fellow, is fatal to the glamour of all artistic work, robbing it of all suggestiveness, destroying all illusion. You seem to believe in literalness and explicitness, in facts and also in expression. Yet nothing is more clear than the utter insignificance of explicit statement and also its power to call attention away from things that matter in the region of art. [CTAF, 142]

Discovering 'the ideal value' of things, events and people seems, therefore, to be a question of removing the 'particular' from actuality, and leaving behind some sublimate which Conrad, using a favoured word, calls 'glamour'.

This is confirmed by a later letter of Conrad's to Curle, in which he outlines the sort of thing that he would like Curle to write about him and his work:

Suppose you opened by a couple of short paragraphs of general observation on authors and their material, how they transform it from particular to general, and appeal to universal emotions by the temperamental handling of personal experience? [CTAF, 195]

This transformation of particular to general is what we see taking place in the Marlow stories, as the very act of narration 'generalizes the particularity' of Marlow's experiences.

But surely, it may be countered, literature is not a series of generalities! Surely one of the things that interests us about a novel is the succession of particular experiences and events that are recounted. Conrad may object to Curle's giving the name of the actual port in *Youth*, which is 'a damned hole without any beach and without any glamour', but the *events* of that tale are particular enough. The point is an important one, for it is at the heart of the way in which literature, and particularly the novel, works. The mistake is to think that the particular and the general are necessarily in total isolation one from the other. Of course, as Conrad points out, some 'facts' may detract from the 'glamour' of art; but again an author can transform the particular in his work so as to give it a general significance. Brecht says that the realist work should be 'concrete and so as to encourage abstraction';[3] writing about *Wuthering Heights*, Arnold Kettle claims that, like all the greatest works of art, it 'is at once concrete and yet general, local and yet universal'.[4]

Let me give an illustration here – and a non-literary one. Fiction is not just novels, and can be found in a wide range of human activities and products. Early on in this book I quoted from James Britton's introduction to Luria and Yudovitch's

3 John Willett (ed.), *Brecht on Theatre*. Eyre Methuen, London, reprinted 1974, p. 37.
4 Arnold Kettle, *An Introduction to the English Novel* I. Hutchinson, London, reprinted 1962, p. 152.

Speech and the Development of Mental Processes in the Child.
In this same introduction, Britton notes that as the child acquires
the ability to use language it becomes possible for it to represent
in words 'what might be' rather than just 'what is'. This jump
represents, I would argue, the ability to detach words from
immediate, concrete circumstances, and to manipulate representations apart from what they refer to. Britton notes that such
representations may equally be a *fiction* or a *plan*, and that
sometimes the two will be indistinguishable. In an important
sense all literary fiction has the function of helping us to plan
how we live – whether it is allowing us imaginatively to experience things we will subsequently pursue or avoid, or whether
it is offering us an escape from the concrete experience of
everyday so as to be able to return with a new vision of it. There
is more to fiction than novels: I was reminded of this recently
when I received a folder through the post advertising different
ways of running up debts with a credit card. The folder was
entitled *Life with the Livingsons*, and included various pictures
of a family doing the various household and gardening tasks
that advertising copy-writers assign variously to men and to
women. The text accompanying the pictures read as follows:

> Spring is only weeks away – so many things to do – rooms to be
> decorated, cupboards to be made, gardening to be done.
>   John and Jean Livingson wanted to start early. The difficult part
> was deciding what to buy. The easy part was deciding how to pay – by
> Access of course. John knows that he can spread the repayments over
> the next few months if he wishes; and by buying a lightweight lawn
> mower for Jean, he might even be able to spread the chores!
>   This year, you can make it easy on yourself – by using Access.

Fiction here is used in that way of which Britton speaks – it is
half way to being a *plan*, although a plan for us rather than by us.
Note how the tense changes in the middle paragraph, so that we
drop from a reality in the first paragraph which could apply to
us directly, to that tense which fiction has made its own in which
we can imagine ourselves as other people. Having experienced
how pleasant this would be, we return to the present tense in
order to bring with us the most important aspect of our trip to
Wonderland – using the credit card.
  What is striking is that at the foot of the last page of the folder
a short disclaimer is printed:

> The Livingson family are [sic] fictitious; any resemblance to persons
> living or dead is purely coincidental.

If that were literally true then one might ask why the advertisers
were spending money telling the general public about imaginary

people who bear only an accidental resemblance to them or to anyone else living or dead. Pretty obviously the family is meant to resemble lots of living people fairly closely. However the disclaimer is not just a dishonesty; what it means is that the family is not intended to resemble a particular family: what it actually resembles is *the particularity of many families*. There is no one family whose members have these names, indulge in these sexually stereotyped household and gardening activities, and use their credit cards to remain solvent. But there are many families (and the advertisers presumably hope that there will be more as a result of the folder) which resemble this imaginary family, or think they do, in a number of ways. Fiction synthesizes the general and the particular, drawing the former out of the latter, not by a naturalistic copy of a given particular fact; but by reparticularizing generalizations and abstractions that have been formed from many particular facts. Conrad's criticism of Bennett, I suspect, is that Bennett has not reached a sufficiently generalized truth before reparticularizing it. This is why Bennett's novels stop short of the real: they are 'true' on one level only.

This working at different levels of generality and particularity gives literature, I would argue, a unique value. It has the value of imparting general truths, but it has validating and corrective links with the particular which defend it from some of the vulnerabilities of generalization and abstraction. If, as Conrad suggests in the letter of his which I have already quoted, Nostromo the character is 'embodied vanity of the sailor kind', he is also a particular individual in the context of the novel who has to behave in a way consistent with his revealed characteristics and circumstances. If Conrad's idea of what 'vanity of the sailor kind' was had happened to have been incorrect, he would have found it very difficult to embody it in the particular form of Nostromo.

In a letter to Edward Garnett written on 11 October 1897, Conrad considers why his tale *The Return* had failed as a work of art. His main explanation is that it had been a mere vehicle for the illustration of an 'idea':

> All this I feel, I don't see; because if I did see it I would also see the other way, the mature way – the way of art. I would work from conviction to conviction – through inevitable moments to the final situation. Instead of which I went on creating the moments for the illustration of the idea. [LFC, 98]

It is as if the successful novel takes a set of particular people and a particular situation which have a general significance, and then allows the internal logic of these particularities to work itself out towards larger general implications. In the unsuccessful novel the particularities have no internal logic of sequence or coherence, but are merely the illustrations of an idea. Whereas the successful novel cannot be reduced to its 'idea', or prose argument, the unsuccessful one can. There are, as Conrad rightly indicates, no 'inevitable moments' in *The Return* – as there are, say, in *Nostromo*.

Thus I disagree with P. N. Furbank's argument in his *Reflections on the Word 'Image'* that, whereas painting works with the particular, 'a given goldfinch in a given cage occupying a given relationship to the wall behind',

> literature works with the general – with words, like 'goldfinch' and 'cage' and 'wall', which stand for classes of things – for all goldfinches, all cages, all walls, however different.[5]

Furbank is right that literature does work with the general, with *ideas* as well as *things*, but I would have thought that words in a work of literature clearly have a more particular reference than to classes of things – sometimes at least, if not always. If the poet could only refer to all goldfinches in a poem then it wouldn't be much use writing a poem about a goldfinch. Furbank is arguing against the position that poetry gives us 'images' of particular things rather than generalizations and ideas. I would argue that it gives us both. There is an interesting section in A. R. Luria's book, *The Mind of a Mnemonist*, in which the author points out that his extraordinary subject, who seems to have thought almost exclusively in graphic rather than conceptual terms, couldn't cope with poetry. Luria comments:

> Many people think that poetry calls for the most graphic kind of thinking. Yet, upon analysis, this idea seems doubtful, for poetry does not evoke images so much as ideas. The images in a poem merely serve to clothe meaning, the underlying intention of the poem. Hence, to understand a poem, we must be able to grasp the figurative meaning suggested by an image.[6]

But if literature does not just give us images, it does not just give us ideas either. Who could reduce the scene where Nostromo discovers Hirsch's hanging corpse to ideas, to generalities? As Dr Leavis has pointed out to us, literature is not philosophy; literature is not just ideas expressed in the 'medium' of words, and it cannot adequately be reduced to its ideas. If it can, as

5 P. N. Furbank, *Reflections on the Word 'Image'*. Secker and Warburg, London, 1970, p. 7.
6 A. R. Luria, *The Mind of a Mnemonist*. Cape, London, 1969, p. 120.

Conrad points out with regard to *The Return*, it is not successful literature.

To return to my own starting point in this chapter, however, it does not necessarily tell us where precisely the other end of the thread is attached merely to say that literature is a complex reparticularization of the general. What Conrad seems more and more to include within his novels up to *Under Western Eyes* is a reminder to the reader that he or she must discover in his or her own life and experience where these threads are attached. In *Under Western Eyes*, as we will see, Natalia eventually returns to Russia, to 'flesh out' her words in experience. In many highly complex ways the novel reminds the reader that he or she is reading words, not experiencing life directly, and that it is up to the reader similarly to flesh out the reading experience.

6

Under Western Eyes: words and visions

Writing has this disadvan[ta]ge of speaking. One cannot write a wink, or a nod, or a grin, or a purse of the Lips, or a *smile* – *O law*!

John Keats, *Letters*

Criticism is very much a matter of a vocabulary, very consciously used; with us it was the intonation that mattered. The tone of a grunt could convey an infinity of meaning between us.

Joseph Conrad, Introduction to
Thomas Beer, *Stephen Crane A Study
in American Letters*, LE, 110

A writing may be lost; a lie may be written; but what the eye has seen is truth and remains in the mind!

The Lagoon, TOU, 194

As Keats points out so well, writing is more abstract than speech, cut off from those other aspects of expressive behaviour which intermingle with speech and contribute to its richness and flexibility. Writing has to look after itself; it cannot rely on the benevolent protection of other sign-systems or on the determining presence of an immediate context. To repeat Vygotsky's words, it is speech in thought and image only, lacking the musical, intonational and expressive qualities of oral speech. He also notes that because it requires a second-order degree of symbolization – that of the sound image in written signs – it is as much harder for children to acquire than speech, as algebra is than arithmetic.[1] Because speech involves more than one person (or 'inner voice') talking about something, it is less monolithic than writing, constituting part of the collective relationship between people and their environment.

In *Under Western Eyes* Razumov changes from an individual who engages little in conversation – and then half-heartedly – and who writes highly abstract academic essays, to one who writes secretly to himself and others and engages in deliberately misleading conversations, but who ends up 'talking well' and

1 TL, p. 99.

apparently writing little. All the way through *Under Western Eyes* language is scrutinized in both its spoken and its written form, and this scrutiny extends to the language use that the novel itself constitutes.

My introductory quotations all raise disadvantages connected with writing: it is without those subtler forms of non-verbal expression that accompany speech, it can tell lies whereas 'what the eye has seen is truth', and it lacks the economy of speech between two friends where a grunt may suffice to convey significant meaning. Yet all of these disadvantages are brought to us in writing. Whatever its disadvantages, writing can talk about them. If speech is honest, rich, and economical, it is also possessed of certain shortcomings. If speech has the reliability and economy that come from its being a part of social interaction in a defining context, it also has the limitation that it cannot always be removed from this defining context without loss of meaning. If it is – and in an age of telephones and tape-recorders this is now possible – it is unable to look after itself in the way that writing, for all its disadvantages, can. It is precisely the ability to detach itself from concrete situations over and above that already enjoyed by speech that makes writing both indispensable and also more dangerous. Its greater degree of abstraction brings with it yet more power and yet more vulnerability to error. But it can talk about these problem: like speech, it can detach itself from itself, and achieve a degree of self-consciousness, so that in its travels it can carry with it a built-in warning against its weakness. This, as we will see, is one of the central concerns of *Under Western Eyes*.

In the novel three main areas of communication and knowledge are scrutinized – writing, speech, and non-verbal (person to person) communication. Not only does the novel attempt to answer that central question of Razumov's 'how can you tell truth from lies?' – a question that relates primarily to the interpretation of messages, particularly written ones; but it also concerns itself with an allied if never-stated question, 'how do we distinguish the real from the imagined?' As I have suggested before, such questions do not just involve the 'plot' of the novel. They involve questions about this novel's status as an object of knowledge and a communicative medium which mediates between writer and reader and reveals something about the world. My own conviction is that of all Conrad's novels this is the most deeply felt, and that in his grappling with these questions Conrad is also grappling directly with the usefulness and morality of fiction itself, with, in short, the worth of his second vocation.

Although *Under Western Eyes* is much concerned with words, its title mentions eyes. The eye both sees and is seen: it is that most delicate organ of sense that knows no guile; its search for knowledge cannot be hidden from others, who are free to interpret its movements. At some point or other in *Under Western Eyes* there is a description of the eyes of almost every character. We learn that a watchman disliked Haldin's 'ugly eyes', that Ziemianitch's eyeballs blinked all white in the light when he was found drunk by Razumov, that General T has pale blue eyes, that Mr de P- has 'insipid, bespectacled eyes', that the 'long bony student' has black, lack-lustre eyes, and that although Mikulin has a mild gaze his eyes are big, with heavy eyelids. Prior to her knowledge of Haldin's death his mother's eyes, we are told, were 'kindly', and all the way through the novel there are references to his sister's trustful eyes. In striking contrast are Peter Ivanovitch's concealed eyes, shielded from others by his sinister dark glasses. A deleted reference in Conrad's manuscript of the novel refers to the 'incessant weak blinking of inflamed eyelids' seen by Razumov behind these glasses [UWEM, 458]. Of his 'benefactor', Madame de S –, we learn that her eyes, though shining, are lifeless 'as though they were as artificial as her teeth' [UWE, 225].

These references are clearly meant to indicate something about the characters concerned, and can be considered in the light of a long tradition of attributing a moral significance to physical appearance. Because the eye is so intimately and necessarily related to communication and knowledge, comments about a character's eyes symbolically implicate both the objectivity or otherwise of their knowledge, and the honesty or otherwise with which they communicate with other people. Ziemianitch's white eyeballs can be taken as an indication of his general non-receptiveness to sensation and knowledge, and perhaps of the passivity and irrationalism of the peasantry in general. Peter Ivanovitch's dark glasses are redolent of hypocrisy and bad faith, and call to mind the eye shade worn by Razumov on his visit to meet Councillor Mikulin at, appropriately, the oculist's shop. The most overt statement in the novel about a relationship between the eyes and the moral identity of their possessor is found in Razumov's statement to Natalia at the end of the novel:

> Of you [Haldin] said that you had trustful eyes. And why I have not been able to forget that phrase I don't know. It meant that there is in you no guile, no deception, no falsehood, no suspicion – nothing in your heart that could give you a conception of a living, acting, speaking lie, if ever it came in your way. [UWE, 349]

What I would draw attention to here is the link between *having no guile*, and *having no ability to detect* guile. Natalia's trustful eyes are the eyes of Eve, innocent and thus unable to detect evil. They reveal her innocence, and they see only innocence. But they also persuade Razumov, eventually, to be innocent – to reveal his guilt to her. Natalia's eyes may entice Razumov's thought to the very edge of the blackest treachery, but they also cause him to draw back from it.

More important than descriptions of characters' eyes in the novel, however, are descriptions of what they do with them. The making and breaking of eye-contact are never casually told in *Under Western Eyes*, but always have a direct relationship with the state of mind and good faith of the characters concerned. It is not to be passed over, for instance, that when Razumov first meets the teacher of languages he stares fixedly at him, but later, when his eyes meet those of the 'worthy opponent', Sophia Antonovna, he looks away from her. At the close of the novel when Razumov is preparing to lie to Natalia about Ziemianitch's responsibility for Haldin's death, he is portrayed with his eyes firmly on the floor until the point at which he prepares to tell her the truth. After hearing his confession Natalia drops her veil and subsequently tells the teacher of languages: 'My eyes are open at last and my hands are free now.'

If the eyes and their movements are indicative of a character's openness and honesty in *Under Western Eyes*, a character's openness and honesty, in their turn, appear to determine how accurately a character can 'see'. 'Seeing right' is associated with open human intercourse throughout the novel, whereas 'seeing wrong' – in the sense of misperceiving people, events and objects – is continually associated with denials of human solidarity. It is as if the refusal to look one's fellows in the eye leads to an inability to see. The more a character in the novel acts selfishly and denies his or her fellow human beings their full humanity, the more subject he or she is to hallucinations and misperceptions. It is as Razumov is deciding to betray Haldin that he has a vision of him lying in the snow. It is after a long process of self-isolation that Mrs Haldin ends up expecting to 'see' her dead son, and believing that he is alive. A readiness for, and vulnerability to, illusion, is seen to be bound up with the moral culpability of preferring subjective fantasies to objective knowledge. The more a person knowingly flees from the truth, the less he or she knows what the truth is. Thus the teacher of languages objects to Mrs Haldin's obstinacy in 'her mute distrust of her daughter', and her illusions, her muteness and her distrust are inseparably connected.

Of particular importance is Conrad's suggestion in the novel that to cut oneself off from other people is to diminish one's ability to know and understand the world. Knowledge is thus presented as a collective rather than a private achievement, for the more characters conceal their inner thoughts and feelings from others the more they lose the ability to 'see', to distinguish truth from falsity. After Razumov has encouraged the pathetic but sincere Kostia to rob his loving father in the mistaken belief that he is helping a threated Razumov to escape from Russia, Razumov finds that his own hold on reality is loosened:

> 'It's a dream,' thought Razumov, putting the little parcel into his pocket and descending the stairs; 'nobody does such things.' [UWE, 315]

In a similar situation alone on the little island in Geneva where he is living a lie – and writing a report of his activities – Razumov, accompanied, ironically, by the statue of the author of the Social Contract, starts to wonder whether life is just a dream and a fear.

Conrad had himself visited Geneva, and had revised *The Secret Agent* there, and I must admit to the critical weakness of wondering whether this work was carried on next to that same statue by which Razumov composes his report. For if the result of being cut off from direct and frank contact with others is to become prey to hallucinations and visions, what effects does his or her own isolation have on the writer? For Conrad, one is tempted to answer, the effect appears to have been similar to Razumov's hallucinations. Writing to E. L. Sanderson on 12 October 1899, Conrad talked of his creative efforts in depressed terms which are very reminiscent of Razumov's Geneva experiences:

> And oh! dear Ted, it is a fool's business to write fiction for a living. It is indeed.
> It is strange. The unreality of it seems to enter one's real life, penetrate into the bones, make the very heartbeats pulsate illusions through the arteries. One's will becomes the slave of hallucinations, responds only to shadowy impulses, waits on imagination alone. And one goes through it with an exultation as false as all the rest of it. [JCLL I, 283]

The production of hallucinations by fiction (lying) in Razumov is paralleled by the production of hallucinations by fiction (literary creativity) in Conrad himself. The unreality of *Under Western Eyes*, on the evidence of Jessie Conrad, did actually enter Conrad's own real life after he finished writing it. Writing to David Meldrum on 6 February 1910 she informs him:

> The novel is finished, but the penalaty [sic] has to be paid. Months of nervous strain have ended in a complete nervous breakdown. Poor Conrad is very ill and Dr Hackney says it will be a long time before

he is fit for anything requiring mental exertion. . . . There is the MS. complete but uncorrected and his fierce refusal to let even I touch it. It lays on a table at the foot of his bed and he lives mixed up in the scenes and holds converse with the characters.

I have been up with him night and day since Sunday week and he, who is usually so depressed by illness, maintains he is not ill, and accuses the Dr and I of trying to put him into an asylum. [LBM, 192]

The parallel with Razumov's case is striking – months of nervous strain, living in a separate world of his own thoughts communicated to himself in writing, ending up with an inability to separate fact and fiction and a feeling that there is no one to whom he can turn. Conrad's depiction of the relationship between free and open communication with others, a firm grasp on reality and an ability to distinguish it from illusion, and human solidarity, certainly seems to owe much to his own experience of writing. In an earlier chapter I quoted Conrad's account of the real world breaking into the developing world of *Nostromo* in the shape of his wife's visitor; here we have evidence of the fictional world breaking into the real one. 'One's will becomes the slave of hallucinations.'

It is not just Razumov whose hold on reality is affected by the impoverishment of his words when they are denied their proper role as openly expressive of his thoughts, in particular situations, to other people. The teacher of languages too is forced to deal with words abstracted from concrete situations and direct human intercourse. The words he teaches are artificially isolated from a vigorous life in actual human discourse – and although the teacher of languages often observes such discourse, he rarely partakes in it.

Peter Ivanovitch, too, uses language apart from concrete situations. Writers are not an admired class of people in the world of Conrad's novels, although they are normally a slightly more favoured group than are journalists. The denial of communicative reciprocity that Peter Ivanovitch's dark glasses seem to represent is related to his being a famous *writer*. As we will see later, Peter Ivanovitch's habits of speech and writing comment upon each other, and confirm that hypocrisy suggested by his dark glasses.

A key factor in Conrad's suspicion of writing appears to be its *one-sideness*. Vygotsky's point that it is speech without an interlocutor is important, for, as we see, whenever he is with an interlocutor Razumov is drawn towards the truth, both in terms of revealing it and perceiving it. For Conrad solitary perception seems almost to be a morbid condition, while dialogue or conversation are the means whereby truth is revealed by and to human beings. Razumov is most in danger of betraying himself when he is talking to another character, whether it be Mikulin, Sophia Antonovna, or even the obtuse Peter Ivanovitch. For all Conrad's expressed distaste for Dostoyevsky it seems likely that the interrogatory scenes in *Crime and Punishment* contributed much to *Under Western Eyes*. One of the obvious, but easily forgotten, things about visions and hallucinations is that they are experienced by individuals, not normally by groups. And as Razumov tells Mikulin, visionaries inspire in the mass of mediocre minds a disgust of reality. Is writing just another form of visionary hallucination? Does it too inspire a disgust of reality in readers? Throughout *Under Western Eyes* that feeling of separation from events experienced by the teacher of languages, to which frequent reference is made, seems to result from his different age and culture and his artificial use of words, and seems on occasions to suggest the sort of separation from real and fictional events felt by the writer.

For Conrad the world of the novel and the real world seem to have been similarly distant from the writer. The writer mediates between the two, but is a full participant in neither. Like a writer the teacher of languages can watch but cannot participate in many of the events he witnesses. A passage in Conrad's manuscript, deleted subsequently, comments from the teacher of languages's point of view on

> how helpless and anxious it made me feel, with the sense of living in another world where only my eyes could follow her and watch that fate as if from an immense distance. [UWEM, 688]

Like Conrad's description of 'Chester and his antique partner' in *Lord Jim* – 'as if reproduced in the field of some optical toy' – the above passage could be describing the writer's feelings towards his characters, able to observe them but not to converse with them. The teacher of languages is, notwithstanding his frequent protests to the contrary, a writer. It is from his pen that what we read ostensibly stems. His feeling of separation from Natalia and Razumov is suggestive of a larger feeling of separation from the full humanity of his characters that is felt by the novelist. The published version of the novel also testifies to this same feeling of isolation on his part:

> [Razumov] had lowered at last his fascinated glance; she too was looking down, and standing thus before each other in the glaring light, between the four bare walls, they seemed brought out from the confused immensity of the Eastern borders to be exposed cruelly to the observation of my Western eyes. And I observed them. There was nothing else to do. [UWE, 346]

Many references to significant eye contact between the teacher of languages and Natalia which appear in Conrad's manuscript are deleted from the published text of the novel, leaving in the main only references to unreciprocated observation on his part. It is as if by doing this Conrad wished to underline not the narrator's interaction with other characters, but his inability to do much more than to observe them. One exception to this pattern comes at the point in the novel when the teacher of languages brings the newspaper report of Haldin's death to his family. The narrator finds that he can 'get hold of nothing but of some commonplace phrases, those futile phrases that give the measure of our impotence before each other's trials', but a few moments later Natalia looks at him 'steadily for a moment', and then starts to cry. As she says to his later comment that he has done little else but look on, 'there is a way of looking on which is valuable', adding that because of it, 'I have felt less lonely.'

Conrad's choice of a teacher of languages as narrator is clearly a considered one. Apart from anything else it allows for an expatiation on the nature of words on the first page of the novel which sets the scene for one of the important enquiries the reader has to be prepared for:

> Words, as is well known, are the great foes of reality. I have been for many years a teacher of languages. It is an occupation which at length becomes fatal to whatever share of imagination, observation, and insight an ordinary person may be heir to. To a teacher of languages there comes a time when the world is but a place of many words and man appears a mere talking animal not much more wonderful than a parrot.
> [UWE, 3]

Words – the material of which the novel is constituted – are thus called into question right from the start. Writing here is made to carry a sign round its neck which reads: 'Do not trust me!'

Towards the end of the novel, while Razumov is talking to Sophia Antonovna, she is portrayed looking at him 'not as a listener looks at one, but as if the words he chose to say were only of secondary interest'. Sophia Antonovna, it would appear, believes with Conrad that 'what the eye has seen is truth.' For the teacher of languages this check on verbal reliability is lost: unconcerned with those non-verbal and paralinguistic aspects of person-to-person communication, he must concentrate on words alone, as must the writer who has no contact with the reader other than through those words. Both the teacher of languages and the novelist examine words out of concrete situations, abstracted from immediate human intercourse. Just as the parrot which shrieks 'Viva Costaguana!' in *Nostromo* reminds us that there are men who use political slogans in the same mindless way, so too the reference by the teacher of languages to man as a talking animal not much more wonderful than a parrot reminds us of the treacherous portability of the word. It is no accident, surely, that the journal edited by Julius Laspara in *Under Western Eyes* is entitled the 'Living Word'. We can presume that like those 'rousing' journals sold by Mr Verloc it will contain few words that are truly living, that convey a human sense of a reality beyond themselves. We are told too, in close succession, that Peter Ivanovitch's eyes are hidden by his dark glasses so that there is 'an utter absence of expression' on his face, but that 'all Europe was aware of the story of his life written by himself and translated into seven or more languages.' In the presence of other people he communicates nothing, but in his books he tells the story of his whole life.

This contrast between his living and his literary presence is made more pointed by quotations from his flowing prose (both printed and spoken), and descriptions of his halting, painful assembling of words in the process of literary composition. Although he is described as eloquent in his writing (a word which, in Conrad's novels, should alert our suspicions), Conrad presents an extract from his famous book in a heavily ironic manner:

> 'My fetters' – the book says – 'were struck off on the banks of the stream, in the starlight of a calm night by an athletic, taciturn young man of the people, kneeling at my feet, while the woman like a liberating genius stood by with clasped hands.' Obviously a symbolic couple. [UWE, 124]

Peter Ivanovitch does not, however, treat Tekla as a liberating genius or as a representative of the people, and she is appalled to find that, although his books are so eloquent, when writing them he gropes for words as if he were in the dark as to what to say. The contrast is not just with his normal 'volley of words' in conversation, but with the effect of his writing, which like Kurtz's report misleads the reader about its creation and its creator. Another deleted passage from Conrad's manuscript makes the point even more explicit:

> [Tekla] had discovered that great phrases were built up laboriously word for word, not in the heat of conviction but with a cold regard for effect. The toil of literary composition seemed to her an horrible, artful [? ? ?] of mere sounds. [UWEM, 644]

The particular meaning that words assume in speech is conditioned by the mode of their selection and delivery: in written books the reader can flow over words in ignorance of the ease or difficulty with which they have been found and put together. The published text of the novel contains quite explicit statements by Tekla contrasting the laboured production of books with their final appearance of smoothly flowing thought:

And their books – I mean, of course, the books that the world admires, the inspired books. But you have not been behind the scenes. Wait till you have to sit at a table for a half a day with a pen in your hand. He can walk up and down his rooms for hours and hours. I used to get so stiff and numb that I was afraid I would lose my balance and fall off the chair all at once. [UWE, 146]

After taking down Peter Ivanovitch from dictation for two years, it is difficult for me to be anything. First of all, you have to sit perfectly motionless. The slightest movements you make puts [sic] to flight the ideas of Peter Ivanovitch. You hardly dare to breathe. And as to coughing – God forbid. Peter Ivanovitch changed the position of the table to the wall because at first I could not help raising my eyes to look out of the window, while waiting for him to go on with his dictation. That was not allowed. He said I stared so stupidly. I was likewise not permitted to look at him over my shoulder. Instantly Peter Ivanovitch stamped his foot, and would roar, 'Look down on the paper!' It seems my expression, my face, put him off. [UWE, 147]

Reading Borys Conrad's account of his father's habitual method of giving dictation to a secretary, it is hard to avoid the suspicion that Peter Ivanovitch represents aspects of his own creative activity of which Conrad was profoundly suspicious:

[Conrad's secretary's] name was Miss M. Hallowes and the fact that my father not only tolerated her presence in the house but even developed some affection for her, was due, I believe, solely to the fact that she was a good typist and possessed the ability to sit quite silent and motionless in front of her machine, hands resting tranquilly in her lap, for long periods, reacting promptly to a word, a phrase, or a sudden outburst of continuous speech, hurled at her abruptly as he prowled about the room or sat hunched up in his big armchair, as he dictated directly onto the typewriter.[2]

Did she, perhaps, share Tekla's disappointment at the contrast between literary composition and the finished book?

Conrad at one point in his manuscript is explicit in contrasting the reliability of direct person-to-person speech with the unreliability of writing. The teacher of languages remembers

also that men who invented speech excusably from necessity have in their wantonnes [sic] come to use it for pleasure, with no aim, for the

2 Borys Conrad, *My Father: Joseph Conrad*. Calder and Boyars, London, 1970, p. 14. Eloise Knapp Hay points out that Conrad's manuscript of *Under Western Eyes* gives incontrovertible evidence that Peter Ivanovitch was meant to resemble Tolstoy in various ways (*op. cit.*, pp. 283, 284).

sound – for the utterance of 'general ideas'; and that this man [Peter Ivanovitch] who aspired to the position of the modern Mazzini had been unreasonably encouraged to talk at large in his books to strangers of many nations. [UWEM, 612]

The theme is a familiar one: speech 'for necessity' is excusable. Not only this, but speech between people who need to use it is likely to be reliable. To talk at large to strangers of many nations in books is a different matter, as those who read them have no ways of checking on their veracity. There is a nice point made in *Under Western Eyes* concerning Peter Ivanovitch's coming across the woman whose husband strikes off his fetters. At this point we are told he had not heard the sound of his own voice for six weeks, and 'it seemed as though he had lost the faculty of speech.' But his restoration to humanity through her cry of profound pity is given in his book 'with a very effective eloquence'.

Conrad seems himself to have experienced particular difficulties in composition while writing *Under Western Eyes*. Writing to Edward Garnett on the 22 August 1908, he told him:

I shall probably take a long spell of heavy pulling at the novel without a name. I have it all in my head and yet when it comes to writing I simply can't find the words, I have been like that before 10 years ago but now it is a more serious portent. [LFC, 226]

Having what you want to say in your head but being unable to find the words is something that happens both when one is speaking and when one is writing. But the difference is that it is apparent in speech: we can see people stuck for the right word, hesitating. Conrad's difficulties in composition seem to have worried him on two levels: firstly the pure and simple worry of whether he would be able to continue earning his bread by his pen, but secondly the dubious morality of producing a text which would read smoothly and eloquently although it had been composed painstakingly.

There may well be other reasons for Conrad's concern with the process of writing in the book. We can remember that in *Lord Jim* Marlow talks of the world outside language which wears a vast and dismal aspect of disorder, and in Jim's semi-articulacy and his final attempt to write down what happened to him there is the suggestion that within individual experience there is also a vast and dismal disorder which is made coherent by words. Vygotsky suggests that experience is something that resides in the individual's consciousness, and that to become communicable it must be 'included in a certain category which, by tacit convention, human society regards as a unit' [TL, 6]. A deleted passage from Conrad's manuscript of *Under Western Eyes* makes a very similar point:

It may be that when Mr Razumov seized the pen it was with the intention of making a resting place for his remembered sensations to the end that they should cease from haunting him in all their force. It does not require the animosity of an old and weary teacher of languages to discover that words are but the grave of all that makes a thought wonderful and an emotion poignant. With the commonplace associations of speech thought becomes acceptable to the commonplace world and the emotion bearable to the relieved soul. [UWEM, 314]

However it should, I think, be remembered that not only were these words deleted by Conrad, but they were also given to the not-totally-reliable teacher of languages. As published the book gives to him statements about the unreliability of speech, but suggests elsewhere that his view is an inadequate one. Razumov, for example, does not find that Haldin's phrase about his sister's trustful eyes is the grave of all that makes a thought wonderful.

Razumov's name, as various critics have pointed out, recalls the Russian word for 'reason'. Prior to Haldin's disruptive bursting into his room and his life, Razumov had lived primarily among books and papers, wrestling with life not so much in terms of pressing material or directly human difficulties, but more in terms of intellectual problems encountered and dealt with through the medium of the written word. Razumov is a social isolate: like the teacher of languages he is unmarried, and at the start of the novel he has no close emotional attachments or relationships. He is of no particular religious or political persuasion, unlike Haldin, and he lacks that love of the spoken word of most of his compatriots who, according to the narrator, pour words out 'with such an aptness of application sometimes that, as in the case of very accomplished parrots, one can't defend oneself from the suspicion that they really understand what they say'. Razumov is not like this; he is

easily swayed by argument and authority. With his younger compatriots he took the attitude of an inscrutable listener, a listener of the kind that hears you out intelligently and then – just changes the subject. [UWE, 5]

Like Conrad himself perhaps, (R. L. Mégroz refers on a number of occasions to his description of himself as 'a reading boy'), Razumov finds that experience with written words does not necessarily prepare one for practical emergencies. He takes a rather superior attitude to the conspirators because of their misuse of language, describing them as

'Fanatical lovers of liberty in general. Liberty with a capital L, Excellency. Liberty that means nothing precise. Liberty in whose name crimes are committed.' [UWE, 50]

His argument here is reminiscent of George Orwell's attack on

W. H. Auden's use of the phrase 'the necessary murder', which Orwell criticized on the grounds that it was clear from the way in which Auden used it that he had no real experience of what murder was like. Auden may believe intellectually that murder is necessary, just as Haldin is committed to an idealized 'Liberty', but neither of them relate this idealized or abstract commitment to the gore and suffering of what it means in practice. Orwell is instinctively suspicious of the abstract, and it can be argued that this often leads him into a naive empiricism or simple-mindedly literal attitude towards the use of language. We all know what a call to revolutionaries to be the hammer not the anvil means, even if Orwell is right that it is hammers rather than anvils which come off worse when the two meet.[3] We can however remember the teacher of languages's point that I quoted earlier from Conrad's manuscript, that men who invented speech 'excusably from necessity' had come to use it for the utterance of 'general ideas'. 'Liberty in general' is perhaps a variant of Peter Ivanovitch's general ideas – an abstract idea which ignores the concrete realities necessary to bring it into being.

It is certainly true that Haldin's use of language is highlighted by Conrad when first he appears in Razumov's room:

> He told Razumov how he had brooded for a year; how he had not slept properly for weeks. He and 'Another' had a warning of the Minister's movements from 'a certain person' late the evening before. He and that 'Another' prepared their 'engines' and resolved to have no sleep till 'the deed' was done. They walked the streets under the falling snow with the 'engines' on them, exchanging not a word the livelong night. [UWE, 17]

Not only do the two use a jargon – perhaps designed for secrecy but certainly acting to conceal the reality of their actions from themselves – but they also exchange not a word on the night of the deed, except when they pretend to be drunken peasants for the benefit of a police patrol. Orwell's point may be naive in some respects (one of the strengths of language is that it can be used without always recalling concrete particularities to mind), but it has a certain relevance to the criticism of the conspirators implicit in the above passage.

But if the reader is expecting to discover that against Haldin's misuse of language we are to consider Razumov's more intellectual usage as acceptable, he is soon disappointed. Razumov may not use language in quite the same way as Haldin, but he does pin up his list of 'general ideas' soon after betraying Haldin. And his attempts at self-justification for his action in betraying

---

3 See, for example, Orwell's essay 'Politics and the English Language'.

Haldin misuse language just as much as do Haldin and his fellow conspirator. What the novel does more and more suggest is that the power of language to escape from the concrete is a dangerous one, and one that should be made use of as sparingly as possible. As I have already argued, Conrad is no simple empiricist: it is worth noting that when Razumov dispenses with language in his encounter with Ziemianitch, and beats him, his blows are as misunderstood quite as much as any words in the novel. The peasant believes that he has been beaten by the devil, and eventually hangs himself. Conrad probably sympathizes with Razumov's dismissal of both 'the drunkenness of the peasant incapable of action' and also 'the dream intoxication of the idealist incapable of perceiving the reason of things'. Conrad sees the need for escaping from concrete experiences, but too long an absence and the escape can become a dream. There is a moving passage in Conrad's essay, 'Certain Aspects of the Admirable Inquiry into the Loss of the *Titanic*', which was published in 1912. Referring scathingly to those designers, managers, constructors and others to whom he gives the collective name of Yamsi, he writes:

> I attach no exaggerated value to human life. But I know it has a value for which the most generous contributions to the Mansion House and 'Heroes' funds cannot pay. And they cannot pay for it, because people, even of the third class (excuse my plain speaking), are not cattle. Death has its sting. If Yamsi's manager's head were forcibly held under the water of his bath for some little time, he would soon discover that it has. Some people can only learn from that sort of experience which comes home to their own dear selves. [NLL, 247]

'Heroes', like 'engines', are spoken of by people who want to conceal realities from their own knowledge, who want to protect themselves from the thought of what drowning is like by a phrase and a contribution.

When Razumov returns to his room after Haldin's arrest it is as if his own head has been held under water for some little time. His books, previously the most important things in his life, now seem to him 'a mere litter of blackened paper – dead matter – without significance'. Faced with the realities of power and death, not to mention brute ignorance on Ziemianitch's part, written words lose their power to signify and revert to a purely material, non-semiological mode of existence. In the opening pages of the novel the teacher of languages remarks that there must be a wonderful soothing power in mere words since so many men have used them for self-communion, and Razumov's reaction to his books after Haldin's arrest is a revulsion against the deceit involved in that soothing power. The time of his deception through the soothing power of words used for self-communion is not yet at an end, however. Razumov has still to learn that it is only when words are used for open communion with others that they can be used for obtaining adequate knowledge of oneself.

I would suggest that Razumov's final confession of guilt is one that is motivated by a realization that until he is open with others he cannot understand himself or his situation. It is a realization that knowledge is obtained through words, the meaning of which has to be forged in use with other people. For the first period of his stay in Geneva he wants to use language as an accurate means of understanding himself, his situation, and other people, while at the same time using it to deceive others about these same subjects. It is arguable that the most important commitment of *Under Western Eyes* is to the irre-concilability of these two aims. Razumov has to choose between deceiving others and himself, or discovering the truth about himself to others and to himself. Through the crisis initiated by his inability to lie directly to Natalia (an inability which is at the same time an inability to go on living in ignorance of himself) he chooses the second alternative.

When Razumov first meets Tekla he is pleased that she is not concerned to be faithful to her employer, and thinks that 'she could be made to talk.' By the end of the novel he no longer wishes to make her talk, but is grateful for her tender care – a care that is reminiscent of the loving concern of another Con-radian character who lacks verbal skill – Stevie. Tekla tells him that she would be willing to bite her tongue out and throw it at 'them', for speech is no longer any use to her: 'Who would ever want to hear what I could say?' Although Peter Ivanovitch's egotism has reduced her to near-speechlessness, to lose all confidence in words, she is able to nurse the deafened Razumov who 'talks well'. She tells Razumov that there is no hope for them, anywhere, unless all the people with names are done away with, and this suspicion of language leads her back to the task of ameliorating suffering directly, much as it leads Natalia in a similar direction. Her mistrust of names stems, we presume, from her ill-treatment by the famous 'name' Peter Ivanovitch, who admires women in the abstract and ill-treats them in practice. Razumov, who at the start of the novel is seeking that distinction that will convert 'the label Razumov into an honoured name', ends up happy to be cared for, rather than spoken of, well. Conrad was presumably particularly conscious of the problematic nature of names not just because he had changed his own, but because he wrote novels in which the characters were just names too for their readers – as indeed he was himself. By ending *Under Western Eyes* with the character who would tear her tongue out caring for the character who has been deafened, some indication of the primacy of direct human contact over the contact mediated through an 'honoured name' is given.

If Razumov is an isolate at the start of the novel, he is isolated yet more by lying. To lie is to separate oneself from other people, rather than to share knowledge with them. Eventually Razumov feels that he must escape his loneliness by betraying himself, as he earlier compounded it by betraying Haldin. Before this point, however, he engages in certain interesting subterfuges to try to maintain his hold on reality. For instance, he tries talking to himself – both in his diary and in inner cerebration. But the results of such 'hidden talk' are far from reassuring. Walking in the Chateau garden with Peter Ivanovitch he lectures himself on the need for caution:

> All sincerity was an imprudence. Yet one could not renounce truth altogether, he thought, with despair. Peter Ivanovitch, meditating behind his dark glasses, became to him suddenly so odious that if he had had a knife, he fancied he could have stabbed him not only without compunction, but with a horrible triumphant satisfaction. His imagination dwelt on that atrocity in spite of himself. It was as if he were becoming light-headed. 'It is not what is expected of me,' he repeated to himself. 'It is not what is – I could get away by breaking the fastening on the little gate I see there in the back wall. It is a flimsy lock. Nobody in the house seems to know he is here with me. Oh yes. The hat! These women would discover presently the hat he has left on the landing. They would come upon him, lying dead in this damp, gloomy shade – but I would be gone and no one could ever . . . Lord! Am I going mad?' he asked himself in a fright. [UWE, 209]

Once thought is locked away from other people, from the pressure of a reality with which it must make contact, then it can become uncontrollable. Razumov discovers that he cannot just go on maintaining a sanity and mental equilibrium while living a lie to other people. Words have to be exercised in the company of other people, or they start to romp around the brain out of control. There is a movement in this passage from an experience which appears to be pre-verbal ('he fancied') to the development of an inner dialogue which is in direct speech in the novel. While the former 'fancies' leads him away from reality into absurd imaginings, the latter brings him back to a realization of his threatening mental instability. Razumov seems impelled towards the truth almost as much by inner dialogue as by dialogue with another person.

Of Gentleman Brown in *Lord Jim*, Marlow tells us that 'if he

was spoken to he was no longer a hunted wild beast.' Peter
Ivanovitch is 'restored to the ranks of humanity' after his escape
from captivity when the woman's 'unexpected cry of profound
pity' discovers 'the complex misery of the man under the terrifying aspect of the monster'. Speech with other people is what
makes us truly human, speech which is part of our shared experience of transforming ourselves and our world. It is this speech
with others that Razumov desperately needs, beyond the tem-
porary expedient of addressing himself in secret. His personal
situation in Geneva is comparable to that of the whole of Russia
which Conrad describes in his essay 'Autocracy and War':

> her soul, kept benumbed by her temporal and spiritual master with
> the poison of tyranny and superstition, will find itself on awakening
> possessed of no language, a monstrous full-grown child having first
> to learn the ways of living thought and articulate speech. [NLL, 102]

For Conrad one of the profoundest accusations that could be
levelled against Tsarist autocracy, both in itself and through the
terrorism that it unwillingly nurtured, was that it murdered
'living thought and articulate speech'. Razumov's thought is not
living, and in an important sense he is possessed of no language.
Language is the means whereby we share the world with others:
Razumov does not – can not – do this. In Geneva he has to learn
the way of living thought and articulate speech.

Razumov tries another way of remaining sane – telling the
truth in such a way that it will not be believed. On a number of
occasions he speaks to the exiled revolutionaries in a deliberately
ambiguous manner. Talking to Peter Ivanovitch, for instance,
he says:

> 'You must render me the justice that I have not tried to please. I have
> been impelled, compelled, or rather sent – let us say sent – towards
> you for a work that no one but myself can do. You would call it a
> harmless delusion: a ridiculous delusion at which you don't even smile.
> It is absurd of me to talk like this, yet some day you will remember
> these words, I hope. Enough of this. Here I stand before you – con-
> fessed! But one thing more I must add to complete it: a mere blind
> tool I can never consent to be.' [UWE, 228]

As Hamlet says to Rosencrantz, 'a knavish speech sleeps in a
foolish ear.' Everything Peter Ivanovitch hears is 'true', but of
course he doesn't have access to this truth. He hears the words
in another way, gives them another meaning, from the true one.
Razumov is like a man who pulls faces while talking to someone
else on the phone, giving vent to the impulsion towards honesty
in a deliberately misleading way. Razumov cannot talk openly
to anyone, so he talks openly to a hypothetical Peter Ivanovitch

of the future, a man who will remember his words and perceive their hidden truth. Razumov wishes to avoid the fate of being a 'blind tool': he wishes to see clearly what he is doing even if it is something he does not want to do. He tells Natalia later on that the blind are best able to look beyond the present, and that he himself had the misfortune to be born clear-eyed. It is to preserve this clarity of vision – threatened by his retreat into the same isolation that causes Mrs Haldin to die in mute distrust, expecting to see her dead son – that he has to speak the truth, even in such a way that it will be misunderstood. His behaviour to Peter Ivanovitch duplicates that to Haldin. After the latter's death Razumov tries to reassure himself: 'I have said no word to him that was not strictly true.' But it's possible to tell lies by saying words that are all 'strictly true'. V. N. Vološinov has written that signs can arise only on interindividual territory:[4] what Razumov learns is that they cannot survive long out of that same environment. We can only learn to speak *socially*, and without open verbal contact with others our ability to use language to understand the world is increasingly impaired.

Towards the end of the novel, talking to Sophia Antonovna, the character upon whom Conrad claimed that, along with Tekla, he had lavished a wealth of tenderness [LFC, 249], Razumov starts to congratulate himself upon his ability to lie to her:

> It gave him a feeling of triumphant pleasure to deceive her out of her own mouth. The epigrammatic saying that speech has been given to us for the purpose of concealing our thoughts came into his mind. [UWE, 261]

In fact, as he goes on talking to her, he finds it harder and harder to deceive her. He is impelled towards the truth in much the same way as he had been in his inner dialogue concerning his fantasy of stabbing Peter Ivanovitch. After she tells him her story he tries hard to raise himself 'above the dangerous weaknesses of contempt or compassion', but later on is moved to the sincere statement:

> 'You are eloquent, Sophia Antonovna ... only, so far you seem to have been writing it in water.' [UWE, 263]

Ossipon too thought that women's words fell into water, but it was the woman who fell into the water and her words which remained to haunt him. Razumov finds that Sophia Antonovna's eloquence is more disturbing than he had imagined it would be. More than this; whereas he is impressed against his will by her

---

4 V. N. Vološinov, *Marxism and the Philosophy of Language*. Seminar, New York and London, 1973, p. 12.

sincere words, she finds his false words to her puzzling, and on two occasions while they are talking she appears to be concentrating more on his non-verbal than his verbal behaviour:

> She had been looking at him all the time, not as a listener looks at one, but as if the words he chose to say were only of secondary interest [UWE, 242]

> He noticed the vacillation of surprise passing over the steady curiosity of the black eyes fastened on his face as if the woman revolutionist received the sound of his voice into her pupils instead of her ears. [UWE, 257]

It is perhaps not irrelevant to note that of course by the end of the novel, as a result of his having been deafened, Razumov is forced to receive the sound of people's voices through his eyes rather than his ears. If the eye is to be taken as a symbol of true perception, this perhaps indicates his having achieved a true knowledge of himself and an ability to communicate freely and openly with others. Early on in the novel he had not been much of a conversationalist, listening rather than contributing to discussion. He then indulges in a sudden burst of loquacity at the point where he is convincing himself to betray Haldin:

> He went on thus, heedless of the way, holding a discourse with himself with extraordinary abundance and facility. Generally his phrases came to him slowly, after a conscious and painstaking wooing. Some superior power had inspired him with a flow of masterly argument as certain converted sinners become overwhelmingly loquacious. [UWE, 35]

Peter Ivanovitch is also 'inspired', and also enjoys an easy loquacity. Such ease of talk is highly suspect, a projection of an inner monologue rather than a genuine dialogue with another person. We are not surprised to read, a page or so after Razumov's burst of loquacity, that he 'longed desperately for a word of advice'. At this point in the narrative a deliberate contrast is drawn between his inner turmoil and his outer calm, and the contrast is representative of his moral vulnerability; for too long he has engaged in dialogue with himself and with books, he is not able to reach that moral truth which we see comes from genuine dialogue with another person. The fact that by the end of the novel he is described by Sophia Antonovna as intelligent, and as one who, 'has ideas. . . . He talks well, too', indicates how much his moral purification is related to a development of communal speech.

Conrad wrote both to Edward Garnett and to Garnett's sister that in *Under Western Eyes* he was concerned, 'with nothing but ideas' [LFC, 249, 251], and although the repetition (he says 'exclusively concerned with ideas' to Miss Garnett) may stem from his having written to both of them on the same day, it is some indication that Conrad was teasing certain problems out in the novel rather than scrutinizing particular characters or situations. Conrad doesn't say what the ideas with which he is concerned are, and we have only the text to go on. Nor is it necessarily the case that his intention is fully realized, or the only significant element in the novel. There are so many references in the novel to language, to the relationship between speech and writing, and to the 'truth' of written reports, however, that I feel fairly confident that some of the ideas with which Conrad was concerned involved the nature of the truth that the work of fiction contained. Robert Alter has argued that Conrad's fiction (he refers particularly to *Lord Jim*) does not have the same degree of self-consciousness as does, say, John Fowles's *The French Lieutenant's Woman*.[5] Other critics have made similar comments on the lack of self-consciousness in Conrad's fiction. Donald Yelton, for example, in his *Mimesis and Metaphor: an Inquiry into the Genesis and Scope of Conrad's Symbolic Imagery*, states the case bluntly:

> Alongside such near contemporaries as James, Gide, Proust, Joyce, and Thomas Mann, Conrad appears to be wanting in artistic self-consciousness and in articulateness about the aesthetics of his craft.[6]

Now it is true that Conrad seems to have been unwilling to enter into long discussions of the meaning of his novels, or to philosophize outside their pages about the aesthetics of his craft. But few novels manifest more consistently than *Under Western Eyes* what Alter defines as the essence of the self-conscious novel – the systematic flaunting of its own condition of artifice which, by so doing, probes into the problematic relationship between real-seeming artifice and reality. One might perhaps jib at the word 'flaunt', but this apart Conrad's novel relentlessly teases away at certain recurrent problems about the relationship between real-seeming artifice and reality. The whole discussion of Peter Ivanovitch's experiences and their literary transformation and dissemination raises questions about the relationship between what we read in a book and the reality of what is described therein.

Any discussion of language, or of narrative – both of which are considered as topics in *Under Western Eyes* – will introduce an element of self-consciousness into a novel. Even the structure of a novel which consists of a narrative within a narrative will raise

5 Robert Alter, *op. cit.*, p. xiii.
6 Donald C. Yelton, *Mimesis and Metaphor: An Inquiry into the Genesis and Scope of Conrad's Symbolic Imagery*. Mouton, The Hague 1967, p. 14.

such self-referential questions, for the questions about one narrative that the meta-narrative involves will reflect back on to the whole novel, to the 'telling' of the author. But in *Under Western Eyes* fictive creation itself is continually made reference to. The first paragraph of the novel takes the form of a disclaimer from the teacher of languages concerning his creative talent:

> To begin with I wish to disclaim the possession of those high gifts of imagination and expression which would have enabled my pen to create for the reader the personality of the man who called himself, after the Russian custom, Cyril son of Isidor – Kirylo Sidorovitch – Razumov. [UWE, 3]

The passage continues in similar vein, ramming home the fact that what the reader is about to read could not have been invented by a novelist, and concluding that the reader would be able to detect in the pages of the novel the marks of documentary evidence even without this declaration of creative incapacity. Many similar passages appear throughout the novel. It is to the teacher of languages that most are attributed.

> In the conduct of an invented story there are, no doubt, certain proprieties to be observed for the sake of clearness and effect. A man of imagination, however inexperienced in the art of narrative, has his instinct to guide him in the choice of his words, and in the development of the action. A grain of talent excuses many mistakes. But this is not a work of imagination; I have no talent; my excuse for this undertaking lies not in its art, but in its artlessness. Aware of my limitations and strong in the sincerity of my purpose, I would not try (were I able) to invent everything. [UWE, 100]

One of the proprieties in the conduct of an invented story is, normally, not to remind the reader that it is an invented story that is being read. By so doing, Conrad does to a certain extent exhibit, if not flaunt, the condition of artifice of the novel he is writing.

Of course there is a long tradition of narrators who disclaim narrative skill in order to obtain verisimilitude, but this passage, and others, seems to go beyond this. What it does is to remind the reader of the fictional nature of what he is reading, that behind the statements of the teacher of languages which, in fictional context, are 'true' are the words of Conrad the author, which are 'false'. Or are they? Is it possible that, taken as the words of Conrad rather than of the teacher of languages, the passage is rather like one of those deliberately ambiguous statements of Razumov's? Conrad put it on record that he lacked the capacity to invent, and it is possible that in such statements as the above he derived the same satisfaction and comfort as did

Razumov. Both the author and his character are forced to speak through a fictional persona; maybe the loneliness of writing affected Conrad much the same way as the loneliness of political deception affected Razumov, bringing with it such a fear of madness that he had to tell the truth – even a truth disguised so that it would be recognized only with difficulty.

In the preface to *A Personal Record* Conrad notes that:

Most, almost all, friendships of the writing period of my life have come to me through my books; and I know that a novelist lives in his work. He stands there, the only reality in an invented world, among imaginary things, happenings, and people. Writing about them he is only writing about himself. But the disclosure is not complete. He remains, to a certain extent, a figure behind the veil; a suspected rather than a seen presence – a movement and a voice behind the draperies of fiction. [APR, xiii][7]

This is published only a year after *Under Western Eyes*, and if Conrad has any particular novel in mind it is quite possibly the one which he has just completed. To me *Under Western Eyes* gives a strong impression of a man talking about himself; behind its draperies Conrad's voice and presence are unobtrusively present. When, at the start of the novel, we see Razumov as a man intending to construct 'his being in the willed, the determined future' [UWE, 77], through his writing, it is difficult to avoid the parallel with Conrad's own life.

It is not just by the reminder of a narrative presence behind that of the ostensible narrator that the novel makes the reader aware of the novel as a novel. In this of all Conrad's novels we are encouraged to detach ourselves from the reading process, to 'separate ourselves from our reading activity', to misquote Marx. Various techniques employed in the novel effect what Brecht achieved in more obvious ways through his so-called 'alienation effect'. Some of these techniques have the same effect on the reader as switching the light on in the middle of a film has on a cinema spectator: we stop existing 'within' the book and start looking at it. The result is that the functions of response and criticism are combined: we respond, and then survey our response.

Let me give one simple example of how this is achieved. At various times the reader of the novel has the impression that he or she is reading a translation. If I can interject a personal note here, I can report that re-reading the novel recently I caught myself half-way to flipping back to the frontispiece of the

7 Hervouet, *op. cit.*, indicates a similar passage to this in the preface to Maupassant's 'Le Roman'.

edition I was reading to see who the translator was. The impression is one that various critics have shared, and when the novel first appeared a reviewer for the 'Atheneum' commented that it was un-English, and read like a translation from some other tongue, 'presumably Russian'.[8] Now this impression may in part be fostered to remind the reader of the problems of communicating over cultural boundaries – an issue that is explicitly raised on a number of occasions by the teacher of languages. But even this can be taken as analogous to the problem of communicating across the gap of time and space spanned by a novel which reaches from writer to many readers.

Very often it is a matter of the tense used. For instance, when Sophia Antonovna is talking to Razumov about Yaklovitch, 'Razumov thought suddenly, "They have been living together."' As Sophia Antonovna has not seen Yaklovitch for many years we presume that what is meant is either, 'They were living together', or more idiomatically, 'They lived (or have lived) together.' We might put this down to an isolated slip of Conrad's – an intrusive Polonism – were it not for other examples. When Razumov is musing about his betrayal of Haldin he considers whether he should go back and confess to Councillor Mikulin:

> Go back! What for? Confess! To what? 'I have been speaking to him with the greatest openness,' he said to himself with perfect truth. 'What else could I tell him? That I have undertaken to carry a message to that brute Ziemianitch?' [UWE, 297]

Again, the forms of the verbs are odd and their unidiomatic ring catches the reader's attention: 'I spoke' and 'I undertook' would be more usual, if we remember Razumov's precise situation at this point, and the above forms are precisely those which might have been used by a foreigner. Razumov is not strictly speaking a foreigner, as he is thinking in his native language (surely) – unless the clumsiness is meant to be that of the teacher of language's translation from his diary.[9]

Let me conclude with two more examples of this 'translator's English' in *Under Western Eyes*. In one of the conversations Sophia Antonovna has with Razumov it is pointed out by the narrator (technically the teacher of languages, although the reader has probably forgotten his narrative presence at this point) that she keeps referring to Razumov as if appealing to a third person. On one occasion when Razumov smiles, she breaks off and says,

8 'New Novels', *Atheneum*, 21 October 1911, no. 4382.
9 Conrad's manuscript has the teacher of languages commenting upon the fact that in the later part of Razumov's journal many passages are written in English, and Razumov himself is portrayed as a pupil of the teacher.

'I should like to know what he is smiling at?' The oddness here is a compound of various stylistic features. Giving a question mark to a statement – perhaps to indicate intonational delivery – is one. Referring to Razumov as 'he', almost as if a third person is being appealed to, is another. In part this may act as testimony to Sophia Antonovna's recognition that Razumov is not engaging in frank dialogue with her, but it certainly·draws the attention of the reader to the words on the page. A final example: when Sophia Antonovna is questioning Razumov about his attendance at lectures on the very 'morning of the deed', she asks him, 'Have you really done it?', rather than, 'Did you really do it?'

These last two examples occur in direct speech while two characters are talking to each other in Russian. The teacher of language may be taking the conversation from Razumov's written account of it, but if so he is translating rather unidiomatically again. We are left with the feeling that the oddness is deliberate, either designed to attract our attention and remind us of the cultural gap between 'Western' readers and the Russian characters, or to highlight the act of translation as symbolic of the problems of conveying meaning in words. Whatever the explanation, these verbal oddities constitute one of the elements of self-consciousness in the novel for the words are not allowed to flow through the reader's mind, but keep catching his or her attention and announcing themselves as words in their own right, not as invisible carriers of meaning.

In my chapter on *The Secret Agent* I commented on Conrad's use of 'free indirect speech'. The technique is important in *Under Western Eyes*, and it is I think another of the methods used to allow the work to comment upon itself. Take the following passage, which moves from a direct speech presentation of 'Madcap Kostia's' to a free indirect speech presentation:

> 'My dad is a very useful man. Jolly good thing it is for me, too. I do get into unholy scrapes.'
> His elation fell. That was just it. What was his life? Insignificant; no good to any one; a mere festivity. It would end some fine day in his getting his skull split with a champagne bottle in a drunken brawl. At such times, too, when men were sacrificing themselves to ideas. But he could never get any ideas into his head. His head wasn't worth anything better than to be split by a champagne bottle. [UWE, 79]

The immediate intention of the technique is, I think, to add an ironic authorial or narrative assent to the words of Kostia. 'Yes, you are no good to anyone, yes you will get your head split one day in a drunken brawl.' But alongside this the style has a sort of cinematic 'panning back' effect; we see first of all just Kostia, then we see the ironic narrator, and we are reminded that it is a novel we are reading.

If such self-consciousness is congealed into the very texture of the language used in *Under Western Eyes*, it is in explicit statements about the art of the novelist that the novel is most effective in modifying what Coleridge called the reader's 'suspension of disbelief'.

> Wonder may be expressed at a man in the position of a teacher of languages knowing all this with such definiteness. A novelist says this and that of his personages, and if only he knows how to say it earnestly enough he may not be questioned upon the inventions of his brain in which his own belief is made sufficiently manifest by a telling phrase, a poetic image, the accent of emotion. Art is great! But I have no art, and not having invented Madame de S-, I feel bound to explain how I came to know so much about her. [UWE, 162]

In Conrad's manuscript version of the novel this passage drew attention yet more directly to the way in which a novelist, as Conrad wrote to Bruno Winawer, 'has to lie constantly, from morning till night' [CPB, 290]. Perhaps even more striking is the fact that after the words 'have no art', in the manuscript, an extra section which exhibits the strings of the puppet yet more strikingly is to be found:

> But I have no art, and in this attempt if I am trying to tell a story I am not certainly [sic] trying to write a novel. I have no inventions in which I could believe myself with sufficient force – not having [&c.] [UWEM, 677]

If Conrad deleted a passage in which the narrator disclaimed the intention of trying to write a novel, he left in a passage in which a character denied that he was a character in a novel:

> 'Upon my word,' he cried at my elbow, 'what is it to me whether women are fools or lunatics? I really don't care what you think of them. I – I am not interested in them. I let them be. I am not a young man in a novel. . . .' [UWE, 185]

A passage like this causes the reader to pause: I suspect that he or she goes through a series of thoughts something like the following: (i) but he *is* a character in a novel; (ii) but he is meant to be the sort of character who is unlike the conventional fictional stereotype of 'a young man interested in women'; (iii) where was I?

In other words, the reader is surprised not by something akin to the lights coming on in a cinema, but more like a character on the screen announcing that he is not a Hollywood actor. It is in this context of a new awareness of the different levels on which words in a novel work that the most important question in the book is posed:

'How can you tell truth from lies?' he queried in his new, immovable manner.

'I don't know how you do it in Russia,' I began, rather nettled by his attitude. He interrupted me.

'In Russia, and in general everywhere – in a newspaper, for instance. The colour of the ink and the shapes of the letters are the same.'

'Well, there are other trifles one can go by. The character of the publication, the general verisimilitude of the news, the consideration of the motive, and so on. . . .' [UWE, 188]

The answer is, I think, a model one. There is no internal guarantee of truth in any piece of printed paper. The colour of the ink and the shapes of the letters are irrelevant: in the technical sense they are utterly arbitrary. It is 'trifles' like the character of the publication, the general verisimilitude of the news and the consideration of the motive that must be taken into account – and no better advice for the literary critic was ever penned by any novelist. The teacher of languages, in a comment on the first page of the novel, may be right that the reader of the novel can 'detect in the story the marks of documentary evidence', but without the trifles of which he speaks later on, this documentary evidence is meaningless. The point is rammed home by the fact that immediately after the exchange between the teacher of languages and Razumov quoted above, the former demonstrates that he has badly misunderstood the letter of Haldin's to Natalia which she has shown him, and assumes on the basis of Haldin's written comments that Razumov was a fellow revolutionist.

What the teacher of languages insists upon is important, his mistake about Razumov notwithstanding. He has an Englishman's suspicion of abstract formulations, and his view that words alone have no guarantee of truth seems to have been shared by Conrad. After hearing Natalia talk of her political ideas and ideals, he admonishes her as a good pragmatical Englishman would:

'I suppose,' I addressed Miss Haldin, 'that you will be shocked if I tell you that I haven't understood – I won't say a single word; I've understood all the words. . . . But what can be this era of disembodied concord you are looking forward to. Life is a thing of form. It has its plastic shape and a definite intellectual aspect. The most idealistic conceptions of love and forebearance must be clothed in flesh as it were before they can be made understandable.' [UWE, 106]

Miss Haldin indeed does flesh out her idealistic conceptions: she returns to Russia, in a manner strikingly reminiscent of the return to Russia of Elena in Turgenev's *On the Eve*, who travels on from Venice to somewhere in that part of the Russian Empire fighting for its liberty, after her husband's death. She goes to tend the sick and wounded with the Sisters of Mercy; Natalia shares her compassionate labours 'between the horrors of over-crowded jails, and the heartrending misery of bereaved homes'. Conrad was an admirer of Turgenev and it is possible that Natalia's return to Russia is modelled on the Russian's heroine;[10] what is certainly true is that in both cases the heroine chooses to leave an unreal situation where revolution and reform are merely spoken about, to the practical work of effecting change where change is required.

If this is the advice of the teacher of language to Natalia, what is Conrad's advice to the reader? My own feeling is that Conrad wished the above advice to stand in both cases. The reader of a novel can 'understand all the words' without understanding what they mean. The novelist can clothe his or her idealistic concep-tions in flesh only up to a certain point. Beyond this point the reader must leave the place of many words that is the novel and clothe these idealistic conceptions in flesh on his or her own.

10 Donald C. Yelton notes that Curle had found resemblances to Turgenev in Conrad's work, and he quotes F. Melian Stawell, 'Conrad', *Essays and Studies by Members of the English Association* VI, 1920, p. 96: '[*Under Western Eyes* is] a work that might have been written by Turgenev.' (Yelton, *op. cit.*, p. 79n). There is also a rather striking parallel to be noted between the two following passages:

'I have never started from *ideas* but always from images.' Turgenev to Y. P. Polonsky, 1892, quoted from Richard Freeborn, *Turgenev: a Study*, Oxford University Press, 1963, by Arnold Kettle in the Open University Course Unit on Turgenev's *On The Eve*, A302 units 10–11, Open University Press, Milton Keynes, 1973, p. 37.

'And also you must remember that I don't start with an abstract notion. I start with definite images and as their rendering is true some little effect is produced' [LCG, 116].

Hervouet, *op. cit.*, p. 485, comments too that 'like Flaubert's, Conrad's natural tendency was to think in images.'

Bibliography

Allott, Kenneth (ed.)
  The Penguin Book of Contemporary Verse. Penguin,
  Harmondsworth, reprinted 1966.
Alter, Robert
  Partial Magic: the Novel as a Self-conscious Genre. University
  of California Press, London, 1975.
Baines, Jocelyn
  Joseph Conrad: a Critical Biography. Pelican edn, Penguin,
  Harmondsworth, 1971.
Bateson, Gregory
  Steps to an Ecology of Mind. Paladin edn, Frogmore, St
  Albans, 1973.
Bernstein, Basil
  Class, Codes and Control I. Paladin edn, Frogmore, St Albans,
  reprinted 1973.
Berthoud, Jacques
  Joseph Conrad: the Major Phase. Cambridge University Press,
  Cambridge, 1978.
Blackburn, William (ed.)
  *Joseph Conrad: Letters to William Blackwood and David
  S. Meldrum*. Duke University Press, Durham, North Carolina,
  1958.
Bohmenberger, Carl, and Hill, Norman Mitchell (eds)
  'The Letters of Joseph Conrad to Stephen and Cora Crane'.
  The Bookman (New York), May 1929, LXIX 3, p. 230.
Busza, Andrzez
  'Conrad's Polish Background and some Illustrations of the
  Influence of Polish Literature on his Work'. *Antemcerale*,
  Rome and London, 1966.
Cockburn, Alexander, and Blackburn, Robin
  Student Power. Penguin, Harmondsworth, reprinted 1970.
Conrad, Borys
  My Father: Joseph Conrad. Caldar and Boyars, London, 1970.
Conrad, Jessie

Joseph Conrad and his Circle. Jarrolds, London, 1935.
Conrad, Joseph
   Collected Edition of the Works of Joseph Conrad, I–XXI,
   Dent, London (see note on these texts, p. vii).
   Holograph of *Heart of Darkness*. Yale University Library,
   consulted in microfilm.
   Holograph of *Under Western Eyes*, entitled *Razumov* but with
   Under Western Eyes written on the last page. Yale University
   Library, consulted in microfilm.
Curle, Richard (ed.)
   *Conrad to a Friend: 150 Selected Letters from Joseph Conrad
   to Richard Curle*. Sampson Low, Marston, London, 1928.
Daleski, H. M.
   Joseph Conrad: the Way of Dispossession. Faber, London, 1977.
Engels, Frederick
   'The Part Played by Labor in the Transition from Ape to
   Man'. in *The Origin of the Family, Private Property and the
   State*, Lawrence and Wishart, London, 1972.
Fleishman, Avrom
   Conrad's Politics. Johns Hopkins, Baltimore, 1967.
Ford, F. M.
   Joseph Conrad: a Personal Remembrance. Duckworth, London,
   1924.
Forster, E. M.
   Abinger Harvest. Penguin, Harmondsworth, reprinted 1967.
Freud, Sigmund
   The Interpretation of Dreams. Translated by James Strachey,
   Pelican revised edn, Penguin, Harmondsworth, 1976.
Furbank, P. N.
   Reflections on the Word 'Image'. Secker and Warburg, London,
   1970.
Garnett, Edward (ed.)
   Letters From Conrad, 1895–1924. Nonesuch Press, London,
   no date [?1928].
Gee, John A., and Sturm, Paul J. (eds)
   Letters of Joseph Conrad to Marguerite Poradowska 1890–1920.
   Translated by the editors, reprinted by Kennikat Press, New
   York and London, 1973.
Glassman, Peter J.
   *Language and Being: Joseph Conrad and the Literature of
   Personality*. Columbia University Press, New York and
   London, 1976.
Guerard, Albert J.
   Conrad the Novelist. Harvard University Press, Cambridge,
   Mass., 1958.

Halle, Louis
  'Joseph Conrad: an Enigma Decoded'. *Saturday Review of Literature*, May 22 1948, pp. 7–8.
Havely, Cicely
  Heart of Darkness. Unit 27 of the Open University Course A 302, Open University Press, Milton Keynes, 1973.
Hay, Eloise Knapp
  The Political Novels of Joseph Conrad. University of Chicago Press, Chicago and London, reprinted 1972.
Hervouet, Yves
  French Linguistic and Literary Influences on Joseph Conrad. PhD Thesis, School of English, Leeds University, 1971.
Hewitt, Douglas
  Conrad: a Reassessment. Third edn, Bowes and Bowes, London, 1975.
Hill, Geoffrey
  King Log. Deutsch, London, 1968.
Hoffman, S. De Voren
  Comedy and Form in the Fiction of Joseph Conrad. Mouton, The Hague, 1969.
Howe, Irving
  Politics and the Novel. Avon Discuss Books, New York, reprinted 1970.
Jean-Aubry, G.
  Joseph Conrad: Life and Letters. Two volumes, Doubleday Page, New York, 1927.
  Joseph Conrad in the Congo. 'The Bookman's Journal' Office, London, 1926.
Kettle, Arnold
  An Introduction to the English Novel 1. Hutchinson, London, reprinted 1962.
  On the Eve. Units 10–11 of the Open University Course A 302, Open University Press, Milton Keynes, 1973.
Kirschner, Paul
  Conrad: the Psychologist as Artist. Oliver and Boyd, Edinburgh, 1968.
Leavis, F. R.
  'Anna Karenina' and Other Essays. Chatto, London, 1967.
  The Great Tradition. Penguin, Harmondsworth, reprinted 1962.
Lidz, Theodore
  The Origin and Treatment of Schizophrenic Disorders. Hutchinson, London, 1975.
Luria, A. R.
  Cognitive Development: its Cultural and Social Foundations.

132   *Joseph Conrad*

Harvard University Press, London, 1976.
The Mind of a Mnemonist. Cape, London, 1969.
Luria, A. R. and Yudovich, F. La
Speech and the Development of Mental Processes in the Child.
Edited by Joan Simon and with a new introduction by James
Britton, Penguin, Harmondsworth, reprinted 1975.
Marx, Karl
Capital 1. Translated by Samuel Moore and Edward Aveling,
Lawrence and Wishart, reprinted London, 1967.
Economic and Philosophical Manuscripts of 1844. Translated
by Martin Milligan, edited and with an introduction by Dirk
J. Struik, Lawrence and Wishart, London, 1970.
Marx, Karl, and Engels, Frederick
The German Ideology, part 1. Edited and with an introduction
by C. J. Arthur, Lawrence and Wishart, London, 1970.
Mégroz, R. L.
*Joseph Conrad's Mind and Method: a Study of Personality in
Art.* Faber, London, 1931.
Minnis, Noel (ed.)
Linguistics at Large. Paladin edn, Frogmore, St Albans, 1973.
Moser, Thomas C.
Joseph Conrad: Achievement and Decline. Harvard University
Press, Cambridge, Mass., 1957.
Najder, Zdistaw (ed.)
Conrad's Polish Background: Letters to and from Polish Friends.
Translated by Halina Carroll, Oxford University Press,
London, 1964.
Nuttall, A. D.
A Common Sky. Sussex University Press, London, 1974.
Pascal, Roy
The Dual Voice. Manchester University Press, Manchester,
1977.
Prucha, Jan (ed.)
Soviet Studies in Language and Language Behavior. North-
Holland, Amsterdam and London, 1976.
Retinger, J. H.
Conrad and his Contemporaries. Minerva, London, 1941.
Rollins. Hyder Edward (ed.)
The Letters of John Keats 1814-1821. Harvard University
Press, Cambridge, Mass., 1958.
Said, E. W.
Joseph Conrad and the Fiction of Autobiography. Harvard
University Press, Cambridge, Mass., 1966.
Sherry, Norman (ed.)
Conrad: The Critical Heritage. Routledge, London, 1973.

Sherry, Norman
   Conrad's Eastern World. Cambridge University Press, Cambridge, 1966.
   Conrad's Western World. Cambridge University Press, Cambridge, 1971.
Sherry, Norman (ed.)
   Joseph Conrad: a Commemoration. Macmillan, London, 1976.
Smith, Barbara Herrnstein
   'On the Margins of Discourse'. *Critical Analysis,* June 1975, 1 5.
Stewart, J. I. M.
   Joseph Conrad. Longmans, London, 1968.
Teets, Bruce E. and Gerber, Helmut E. (eds)
   Joseph Conrad: an Annotated Bibliography of Writings about him. Northern Illinois University Press, De Kalb, Illinois, 1971.
Thorburn, David
   Conrad's Romanticism. Yale University Press, Yale and London, 1974.
Vološinov, V. N.
   Marxism and the Philosophy of Language. Translated by L. Matejka and I. R. Titunik, Seminar Press, New York and London, 1973.
Vygotsky, L. S.
   Thought and Language. Translated by Eugenia Hanfmann and Gertrude Vakar, MIT Press, Cambridge, Mass., reprinted 1971.
Watts, C. T. (ed.)
   Joseph Conrad's Letters to R. B. Cunninghame Graham. Cambridge University Press, Cambridge, 1969.
Willett, John (ed.)
   Brecht on Theatre. Eyre Methuen, London, reprinted 1974.
Wittgenstein, L.
   Zettel. Basil Blackwell, Oxford, 1967.
Yelton, Donald C.
   Mimesis and Metaphor: An Inquiry into the Genesis and Scope of Conrad's Symbolic Imagery. Mouton, The Hague, 1967.

Index